A

BEASTLY

MENAGERIE

A

BEASTLY

MENAGERIE

SIR PILKINGTON-SMYTHE'S
Marvelous Collection of
Strange and Unusual Creatures

LYONS PRESS
Guilford, Connecticut
An imprint of Globe Pequot Press

To buy books in quantity for corporate use
or incentives, call **(800) 962–0973**
or e-mail **premiums@GlobePequot.com.**

Lyons Press is an imprint of Globe Pequot Press.

Library of Congress Cataloging-in-Publication Data

Pilkington-Smythe, Sir.
A beastly menagerie : Sir Pilkington-Smythe's marvelous collection of strange
and unusual creatures / Sir Pilkington-Smythe.
p. cm.
Includes index.
ISBN 978-1-59921-986-8
1. Exotic animals / Pictorial works. 2. Exotic animals / Anecdotes.
3. Exotic animals / Humor. I. Title.
QL73.A1P55 2010
590—dc22
2010011813

Printed in China

Text by Danny Beck
Design by Lindsey Johns

10 9 8 7 6 5 4 3 2 1

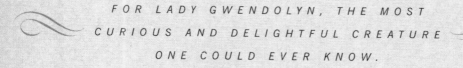

FOR LADY GWENDOLYN, THE MOST
CURIOUS AND DELIGHTFUL CREATURE
ONE COULD EVER KNOW.

CONTENTS

CHAPTER FOUR
REPTILES

CHAPTER FIVE
BIRDS

CHAPTER SIX
MAMMALS

INTRODUCTION

Bobbing around in the vacuum of space is a little dot we call home. Indeed, we're not the only ones who keep our slippers and pipe there; there are all sorts of smashers we are lucky enough to be neighbors with. I'm not just talking about the family dog either—all sorts of weird and wonderful creatures are skedaddling around just outside your window, from worms that eat whales to lizards that eat men, and from snakes that can soar through the sky to flies that can't bloody well fly. There are creatures that can live in the vacuum of space, or even in the head of an ant, and beasts big enough to sink a boat or tiny enough to live on your eyelashes. It is fair to say that there are enough curious creatures on this delightful planet to fill a book … which was rather handy when it came to this publication as it would have been a bit short otherwise.

"WHAT THE BLAZES ARE YOU LOOKING AT?"

Please allow me to introduce myself; Sir Pilkington Smythe at your service: connoisseur, raconteur, *bon vivant*, lover, fighter, and pipe smoker. Please allow me to also introduce the renowned institution to which I and my fellow academics belong: The Proceedings of the Ever so Strange. We are held in remarkable esteem among our learned peers in Blighty (Great Britain to the uninitiated). Not least in my round of introductions I would also like to take the opportunity to welcome you, dear reader; you are clearly a scholar and a gentleman.

This, dear reader, is the remarkable proboscis monkey. Please do turn to page 158 for a closer look.

"I WOULD WAGER FIVE SHILLINGS THAT YOU HAVEN'T A CLUE WHAT THE DEVIL I AM."

Tiny creatures of rather breathtaking beauty abound, such as this charming fellow featured on page 82.

Of course, you are aware that this is our first title, a marvelous menagerie of curious creatures from an insignificant dot in a very big vacuum. Naturally, it was compiled down at the Zoology Department, a department we are particularly proud of for a number of reasons. Zoology is quite simply the study of curious matters pertaining to animals—"weirdness," in a word. Zoology is the study of life, and life is pretty much all we have.

From Humble Beginnings...

Let's go right back to the start. In the beginning there was a right kerfuffle, in which the Earth was formed and almost instantly molecules clunked and clanked into each other to form more complicated ones. These complicated molecules rather remarkably began to make copies of themselves, and thus it was that life appeared on our planet. Soon enough, these little blobby examples of life had formed all sorts of shapes too strange to possibly imagine in today's terms. There were five-eyed blobs that looked like cleaning contraptions, and there were worms on stilts. Among the many ill-suited creatures, there were one or two that actually became rather successful. After many moons on our little planet, living things began to drag themselves out of the wet stuff—little wrigglers to begin with, followed by bigger fish. Seeing the wealth of opportunity that lay before them, they began changing to fit. They made very strange shapes, from froggy to flappy, lizardy to warm and fuzzy.

Not content with being curious, these shapes changed to become curiouser. The froggy shapes grew into giant salamanders and wonderful wormy things. The lizardy shapes turned into miraculous miscreants and blood-squirting horrors. There were birds that turned into vampires and others that made mountains out of their poop. Most upset at how well the others had done, the mammals went all out—they developed magnificent bottoms and learned to make castles with pee, and evolved into boozy shrews and aquatic leviathans that just aren't right. They even turned into upright apey shapes.

I do hope you enjoy our little collection and take a moment to wonder at the peculiar delights that share our insignificant little dot bobbing around in the emptiness of space.

Sir Pilkington-Smythe

CHAPTER

I

INVERTEBRATES

The first lifeforms didn't have a backbone; instead these pioneers sploshed around the oceans in all manner of curious guises. There were the sea urchins, sponges, and jellyfish, and a cornucopia of wigglers too numerous to mention. Some of these got bored of their silly splishing and splashing and began to scamper up onto dry land.

There they had a marvelous time and became decidedly less blobby and altogether more curious. There are insects with a sting that really do sting and bites that make you wish you weren't born. There are spiders that could make Beelzebub blubber, and crabby crustaceans the size of a dog.

The invertebrates … call them what you will, just don't call them spineless.

OCEAN QUAHOG CLAM

ARCTICA ISLANDICA

Deep in the North Atlantic lives a black clam. This swarthy shellfish has quite a claim to fame; he's remarkably old, you see, though don't bother asking him about it because he's completely unaware. Say hello, or don't waste your time saying hello, to the oldest creature on the planet … the ocean quahog clam.

The ocean quahog, also known as the mahogany clam, though he's rather indifferent to what you call him.

Fact

While Arctica islandica *may be the oldest animal ever found on the planet, there are a couple of notable others. There is a type of sponge that lives in the Arctic that is thought to be up to 1,550 years old. There are corals that are thought to live for even longer, though they are in fact made up of hundreds of tiny animals living as a colony. These creatures live and die in much the same way as the cells of our body, so it's wide of the mark to say that they are the oldest living animal.*

For the past four hundred years this clam has sat in the murky deep of the North Atlantic, utterly unaware of the way the world around him has changed.

Lacking the ability to hear is something of a handicap when trying to keep abreast of current affairs, and so he couldn't be told that, while he was starting life, Elizabeth I, with her festering black teeth, sat atop the British throne, and a young William Shakespeare was just putting quill to parchment. He would have seen the pilgrims set sail to New England—to whom he would have presumably said a cordial "How do you do?" as they sailed past—if only he had been able to see. He was unaware when Thomas Jefferson signed the Declaration of Independence and when Beethoven composed his Ninth Symphony. He couldn't give a hoot for a number of landmark events that he lived through, to be perfectly honest … the invention of the telephone, penicillin, the atom bomb, and the First and Second World Wars. Even the parlous state of welfare provision was said to rile him only a tad.

Until one day, researchers from the University of Bangor, Wales, found him in the waters above Iceland that he so fondly called home. There they counted the layers of his shell that had accumulated year after year. Over the centuries he had grown to just 3½ inches (8.9 cm) across, and the researchers counted 405 layers—one for every year of his life. He spent more than four centuries sitting at the bottom of the ocean, blissfully unaware. Of course they killed the poor bugger in the process.

"… STILL NO CURE FOR THE COMMON BIRTHDAY."

The oldest animal in captivity, a Galápagos tortoise, sadly died recently in an Australian zoo at the ripe old age of 175. Rumor has it that she was one of the Galápagos tortoises bundled aboard the Beagle *by Charlie Darwin. Of course, with Galápagos tortoises being notoriously difficult to determine the gender of, and with no one actually taking the time to try, it was only in the last few decades that someone realized that "he" was a she, and Harry soon became Harriet.*

More recently, scientists found an incredible species of jellyfish, Turritopsis nutricula, *that may in fact be immortal. It has the canny knack of being able to revert back to its immature form, so that the adults return to being babies. Furthermore, scientists believe the jellyfish may be able to do it indefinitely, and therefore live forever. Of course, having only just discovered them, it will be a long while before we establish whether they are truly immortal—forever in fact. Fascinating stuff, we are sure you'll agree, though don't waste your time asking the jellyfish about it—he's just as bloody ignorant as the ocean quahog clam.*

The ocean quahog clam is found throughout the North Atlantic, though don't bother going to see them as they are dreadful company.

COCONUT CRAB

BIRGUS LATRO

Gadzooks! It's enormous! Up to six feet across! Say "How do you do?" to the coconut crab, the world's biggest land crab. Just don't try to shake its hand. Unbelievably, this fellow is actually a type of hermit crab—yes, those tiny things you see skedaddling around the shoreline carrying a seashell house on their backs. Of course, the coconut crab would probably need a four-door family hatchback as a house, so it gave up on that idea quite some time ago.

The coconut crab is so-called because it eats coconuts . . . oh, and it's a crab. The thing about coconuts is that they are tough, really bloody tough. And the thing about things that can open up coconuts is that they are strong, really bloody strong. Remarkably, this tenacious crab can crack coconuts by hammering at them with its claw, or, if it's being a particularly tough nut, it will carry it up a tree and drop it onto something hard. Incidentally, the coconut crab isn't the only creature to employ this rather clever tactic; bearded vultures will rakishly use the same technique to open up tortoises. Not great news for tortoises, or indeed for the Greek playwright Aeschylus, who, having fought bravely to smite Persian hordes and drive them from his beloved homeland, was later brained by a falling tortoise.

Enough about the Greeks, let's get back to the chap that eats things that are equally thick and hairy. The coconut crab is also known as the "robber crab" as it apparently has a penchant for petty thievery. Much like Lady Gwendolyn, it's usually rather docile but can be enticed with shiny objects. If you are unlucky enough to have your pocket watch picked by this rascal, I can only advise you to let him have it. "Have you gone soft in your old age, Sir Pilkington-Smythe? You've run many a rapscallion through for much less!" I hear you cry. Well, the thing about the coconut crab is that he's big. Very big. In fact, he's as big as a land animal with a complete exoskeleton can get.

If the coconut crab was, for some unknown reason, sat upright on his *derrière* in this fashion his pincers would come up to your family jewels … which is, of course, the last place you'd want them.

Fact

The biggest crab in the world is actually the Japanese spider crab, a huge gangly thing that can be up to 13 feet (4 m) across—the size of a standard trampoline! It can grow so large because it is supported by water. Thankfully, it has neither the strength nor the inclination to haul itself onto dry land.

Keep Calm and Carry On

If you are ever unlucky enough to be nipped by one of these fellows, it's common practice to scream bloody murder. Of course, that won't be enough to get him to let go, as quite frankly he doesn't give a damn for all your wailing, and if he doesn't want to let go, he won't. Locals, thankfully, have come up with a ploy to get the stubborn crab off—give him a good tickle. The only drawback to this otherwise admirable ploy is that when something that cracks coconuts for a living is attempting to crush your left leg, your natural response is unlikely to be to muster up a big smile, tickle its tummy and say "coochie coo."

Exoskeleton

Exoskeleton refers to the concept of having a skeleton on the outside, rather than on the inside: a shell, as it were. A very sensible idea it is, too. Having the squishy parts on the inside rather than the outside offers a rather effective bit of protection against the elements, and indeed any predator who might think you fair game as a satisfactory brunch. Virtually all adult arthropods have an exoskeleton—that is, all the insects, arachnids, crustacea, and far too many other types of animals to mention here. The trouble is that it's rather cumbersome, which is possibly the only bit of good news about it: because it's so clunky, it fixes the upper limit of how big arthropods can get (which, not incidentally, is why we don't get spiders the size of elephants). I'm sure you will all agree that this small point is rather a relief.

"Replace the stick with your left leg and begin tickling."

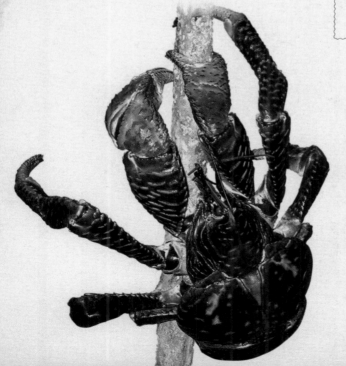

Eating coconuts means that this crab has the rather enviable ecological niche of hanging around on palm-fringed, white-sanded beaches.

TONGUE-EATING LOUSE

CYMOTHOA EXIGUA

The tongue-eating louse is the only example of a parasite that crawls into another animal's mouth and, after dispatching a body part, lives as a rather awkward replacement. It does so with relatively little harm to its host, although it is said the poor bloody fish rarely gets a smooch these days.

This creature is an unwanted guest, like some insufferable bore from college who invites himself over and stays far too bloody long, decimating your wine cellar and not leaving until the day he dies. The tongue-eating louse is quite possibly the most repugnant thing on the planet. He's simply a monster, albeit a little one. The crustacean crawls into the gills of a fish, scrambles up into the mouth and stabs his claws on either side of the fish's tongue. Despite the name, he doesn't actually eat the tongue; the organ atrophies as the parasite slurps the blood, taking with it all the oxygen and nutrients and what-not. There the louse sits for the rest of his life. Why the heck he never evolved to eat the tasty morsels that the poor bloody fish is eating is anyone's guess. We also wonder how he could possibly find this living-in-a-fishy-mouth lifestyle ideal.

> After going through the trauma of having the tongue-eating louse removed, the snapper failed to comment on his predicament.

"It's not ideal, but we do get along marvelously."

Parasitism

Parasitism is a symbiotic relationship with another animal where one animal, the parasite, lives at the expense of another, the host. There are many types of parasitism. Ectoparasites, like the flea, live on the host's surface, while endoparasites prefer it all nice and warm and snuggly inside. Obligate parasites cannot live without their host and, while kleptoparasites steal other animals' food, the brood parasites plop their young into the nest of a host to usurp the host's offspring. There are even epiparasites, which live in other parasites. We don't know if there is a word for obligate endoparasites of ectoparasites who parasitize kleptoparasites who steal from brood parasites.

"Run that by me once again, old bean."

A Slip of the Tongue

So do we at The Proceedings wish we had never mentioned the horrible buggers? Quite the opposite, we think they are really quite grand! An incredible specimen, nay the pinnacle of evolution! You see, parasites rather obviously live off a host, much to the host's detriment. It is an unashamedly lazy, but devilishly clever survival technique that has arisen again and again independently throughout the course of evolution. It is safe to say almost every single animal of any size has at least one parasite for company. The really highly evolved parasites, however, tap the host's resources while allowing it to live on quite normally so that the little devil can tap more and more resources, and make more and more horrible little offspring. We at The Proceedings can think of no other parasite that does it quite so well.

Indeed the closest we could think of is our own offspring, living off the blood of their mother, before popping out to become a bit of a pain until they're eventually packed off to a cripplingly expensive boarding school until they are ready to find some fine pursuit of their own. Which is at least some good news for the parents as they can get back to smooching—a smooch that contains millions of microorganisms, some of which are parasites.

Fact

The tongue-eating louse is usually found off the Californian coast, although it has recently been discovered off the British coast. You can be damn sure it wasn't invited.

Lice are insect parasites found on every single order of birds and mammals (apart from the monotremes). The fish lice however aren't insects— they are in fact crustaceans, and we currently know very little about these fishy fellows. A really rather wise man once said that we will never name all the fish in the ocean, so what chance have we got to name all the tiny things that scrabble about on their skin or indeed replace their tongues?

EYELASH MITE

DEMODEX SPP.

Say hello to the Demodex. *Oh, you're already acquainted … glad to hear it.*
He lives on your face? Of course, how silly of me! In that case may I also introduce
someone who I'm sure you don't know that well: you.

O n the whole we like to think that we know ourselves, whether we
like blondes or brunettes, how we like to take our tea, whether
we prefer a 1795 or an 1818 Château Lafitte Rothschild. Though it
may just be that we don't really know who or indeed what we really
are, or even what we are home to. *Demodex*, also known as eyelash
mites, unsurprisingly live at the bottom of our eyelashes. They are
among the smallest of the arthropods, those armored invertebrates
that include the insects and crustaceans. The eyelash mites are thankfully less noticeable than most arthropods and are in fact only about a
third of a millimeter long, which is probably for the best as nothing
spoils a pretty face quite like a visible infestation of large armored
invertebrates.

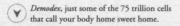

Demodex, just some of the 75 trillion cells
that call your body home sweet home.

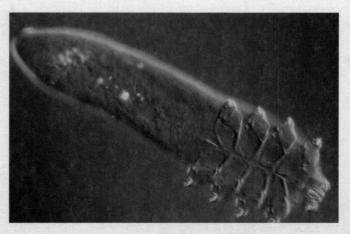

Piggyback, Anyone?

The eyelash mites eat the flotsam and jetsam on your skin: bits of dead flakiness, oily stuff, and so on. They are obviously no bother at all—you'd probably have noticed if they were—and under normal circumstances cause us absolutely no harm, apart from giving us a slight ambivalence toward our lashes. This relationship between two animals is known among learned types as a "commensalism." One genus of animal, in this case the *Demodex*, has a rather good deal out of living with the animal. What's more, unlike say a parasitic relationship, the other animal is completely unaffected by their presence. The *Demodex* to us are like a bird hopping around on a rhino's back, catching bugs, or like a barnacle on a whale's nose. At the end of a hard day, the eyelash mites like nothing better than to go for a promenade around your face while you snooze. Thankfully they are very polite guests, and as their digestive system is so efficient there isn't any waste. Again, this is rather good news as it means you don't have to worry about them using your face as a toilet.

Though it is not for his thoughtfulness that the little mite makes an entry into this fine publication; in fact it is not just him that has captured our rather overactive imaginations. As we alluded to earlier, it may be that you don't know yourself quite as well as you thought. The human body on average contains 10 trillion cells, which is a great many zeros (13 in case you were wondering). In that 10 trillion cells that make up you, there are 75 trillion foreign cells. Yes that is seven-and-a-half times more cells of different creatures living in or on you right now. You are a seething mass of other creatures: parasites, bacteria, fungi, and a rather lovely chap who is no trouble at all, and goes by the *nom de plume* of the eyelash mite.

Commensalism

A commensalism is a form of symbiosis that doesn't always denote a positive relationship—even parasites are symbionts. As well as parasitism, there is mutualism, where everyone wins from the relationship. In commensalism, one animal lives on another but has absolutely no effect on the host—a bit like having someone who isn't hungry around for tea. Indeed, the words *cum mensa* mean "sharing a table."

These tiny creatures can be found anywhere that there are eyelashes, which is pretty much everywhere, then.

HUMBOLDT SQUID

DOSIDICUS GIGAS

These evil buggers are six and a half feet (2 m) long, incredibly intelligent, have tentacles covered in teeth, and swarm in the thousands. They also rather enjoy a chomp on human flesh every so often when they tire of fishy treats, so it is no wonder the natives call them los diablos rojos *(the red devils) and undoubtedly a number of names that aren't quite so polite to boot.*

There are many reports of huge shoals of these devils attacking fishermen, divers, each other, underwater cameras, and anything else that they bloody well want. What is more, the evil sods shoal and attack with their tooth-filled tentacles, grabbing and tearing and pulling you toward their sharp, beak-like mouths, which apparently isn't as much fun as it sounds. Found in the Sea of Cortez and off the coastline of northern Peru, the good news for our North American friends is that they are multiplying and moving northward. So do take care to look around you the next time you take a dip.

El diablo rojo was previously only found off the coast of Mexico, although they are now moving northward up the coast of the USA.

Squid, along with the octopus and the cuttlefish, make up the really rather clever cephalopod family. The cephalopods are in fact mollusks—the same group of animals as snails, slugs, clams, oysters, and mussels. Of course, telling Humboldt squid that they are in fact nothing more than jumped-up shellfish is not very advisable. In fact it borders on the silly. In their short life span, the cephalopods exhibit remarkable intelligence: some use tools, others appear to play, and many display personality traits. Humboldt squid can communicate with one another too. They have chromatophores in their skin, allowing them to quickly change color as a means of talking to each other, rather like a flashing billboard. No one knows what the squid are saying, although it isn't likely to be very nice.

It says, "If you can read me you're too close."

BLUE-RINGED OCTOPUS

HAPALOCHLAENA SPP.

The blue-ringed octopuses are a group of three, possibly four species that dwell in the Pacific Ocean. They may be adorable, but they are also bloody well deadly. These tiny little cutesies each carry enough venom to kill eight humans, and there is no antivenin.

"Angry? I'm bloody vivid mate!"

These eight-legged assassins, despite being delectable and about the size of a golf ball, are deadly—though you wouldn't know it to look at them. At first you probably wouldn't even know they were there, expertly camouflaged as they often are. If you venture close enough to vex them, however, they'll turn a brilliant yellow with bright blue rings—a rather glorious way to tell you that you're in big trouble. If one chomps on you, the array of poisons, created by bacteria in the salivary glands, hits the body from every angle, and within minutes you cannot breathe. Soon enough you cannot move, which also of course stops you from telling anyone about the not-quite-so-adorable-now bugger that bit you, and your ticker eventually does its final ticking. The only hope for you in fact is artificial respiration; if someone works out what is going on, and if they can get you quickly onto some sort of breathing apparatus, then you may survive. If not, you have got about as much chance as a biscuit in a fat man's bed, I'm afraid.

 The blue-ringed octopus is found (unless it's camouflaged, of course) in the seas around Australasia and southeast Asia.

(LEXICON)

Aposematic Coloration

When an animal wants to tell you just how bad it is as a meal it may display vivid coloration, like for example when the blue-ringed octopus turns bright yellow and decidedly more ringy than it used to be. Indeed, a whole host of kaleidoscopic creatures advertise how bloody awful they are to eat, as do these newfangled fast-food establishments, come to think of it.

GLAUCUS

GLAUCUS ATLANTICUS

—◆◆◆—

This blue sea slug is an indubitable beauty, but beneath the beauty hides a savage killer, a femme fatale *as it were. What's more, this seductress eats some of the most feared beasts in the ocean.*

The glaucus is a really rather splendid creature. It belongs to a rather beautiful group called the nudibranchs. These psychedelic slugs, so called because of their naked gills, display their bright colors as a warning of toxicity. It is the story of how the glaucus came to be rather poisonous that propels this coquette into our book. You see, this siren actually eats men alive, really really dangerous men, Portuguese man o' wars to be precise.

As you can see on pages 44–5, the Portuguese man o' war kills most small creatures in his path, and woe betide any human unlucky enough to stray into his tentacle curtain, or indeed the thousands and thousands of tentacle curtains of a swarm. Our siren, the glaucus, will gobble up every single last bit of a Portuguese man o' war, even the venomous nematocysts which collect in little sacs at the end of the feathery protrusions of the body. All of this means that, like most *femme fatales*, it is a very bad idea to try to pick up this temptress.

The glaucus will happily gobble down other members of the pleuston—the unusual creatures that live on the very surface of the sea—and are more than happy to cannibalize one of their own species given half the chance. That is not the only thing that is bizarre about this deadly beauty; she lives in a rather unusual position on the surface of the ocean. No, not floating on top, nor breaking the surface like an iceberg; she is found upside down underwater, stuck to the ceiling as it were. A rather strange and very beautiful *femme fatale*.

"COME UP AND SEE ME SOMETIME."

> **LEXICON**
>
> ## Pleuston
>
> These fellows are the unusual bunch of creatures that live on the surface of the sea. Among their number are snails that bob around on bubble rafts, and the by-the-wind sailor jellyfish that have sails like little boats.

The glaucus' boudoir at the surface of the ocean can be found anywhere warm enough not to be troublesome to her frilly outfit.

TAR-BABY TERMITE

GLOBITERMES SULPHUREUS

———— ·❦· ————

Good grief, these fellows have a worse cuisine than the Scots! Termites, finding that small bits of wood are easier on the mandibles, look upon furniture and other wooden parts of houses as a fine supper. So fine in fact that they cause more than five billion dollars of damage every single year in the United States alone.

Fact

It is thought of as rather rude to mention their relations "the roaches" at a termite soirée.

To say that there are an incredible number of termites in the world is a massive understatement; in fact, they make up about ten percent of the world's biomass. Let's put that into perspective; that's ten percent (by weight) of all the animals, plants, fungi, and bacteria in the world. That includes all of the human race, all the plankton in the sea, and all the blue whales that eat the plankton. It includes the giant sequoia—in fact all the trees, and all the farm animals and crops, all the wild animals and plants, and everything else that's living. Termites make up an incredible ten percent of that rather substantial weight.

It was quite understandably assumed in years gone by that termites were related to that other enormous group of six-legged fiends, the ants. Up until now, that is. Through the newfangled jiggery-pokery of DNA analysis, it has been discovered that termites are actually cockroaches, and today we are having a quick peruse of one particularly social cockroach: the tar-baby termite. You see, this ever so strange creature has evolved a rather effective defense against marauding ants. He quite simply explodes his head, killing himself in the process, and leaving behind a sticky, impassable goo so that his nest-mates can live on. A marvelous example of *kamikaze* in the termite world, and rather commendable to boot, I'm sure you'll agree.

At least nine species of carpenter ant from southeast Asia exhibit the gluey, exploding-head behavior too. What is more, the ants and the termites—being quite unrelated—must therefore have evolved the rather bizarre behavior independently.

"MY HEAD IS GOING TO DO WHAT NOW?!"

You can pop in to see tar-baby termites in the Malay archipelago, though be careful they don't pop themselves.

LEECH

CLASS: HIRUDINEA

These buggers aren't quite the bloodsucking denizens of hell that you might have been expecting. What is more, most of them aren't even bloodsuckers; many eat little creatures that they gobble up whole. Leeches come from the same family as the earthworm—the annelids—so you could say they are no more than a sophisticated earthworm.

While nine out of ten leeches do not have vampirish qualities, the ones that do are fantastically well adapted for the task. Of course it is the bloodsuckers that have ghoulishly captured the public's imagination, in particular the European medical leech (*Hirudo medicinalis*). These slicksters have a sucker at the front that attaches to some poor sod both with mucus and with suction, before three jaws proceed to saw into the skin to open up the capillaries beneath. At this point the cads inject an anticoagulant—though they aren't thoughtful enough to use an anesthetic as is often erroneously thought—and suck up lots of lovely red stuff.

An underhanded fiend he may be, slurping free meals off everyone, but the leech has been used for centuries as a form of medicinal bloodletting. One of the earliest healing techniques was to tap the body's blood, and many different cultures, from Mesopotamia to the Americas, employed the technique. Of course, leeches were used as an easy, portable, and altogether less messy way of doing it. So popular in fact was the use of leeches that they were almost collected to extinction. The job of collecting the leeches was pretty much the worst job that has ever existed, though it was rather simple to roll up your pants and allow them to attach to your legs. As many as 2,500 could be gathered in a day.

Fact

If you are unlucky enough to be bitten by a leech it is a very bad idea to stab it, burn it, put salt on it, or whatnot. This simply causes the leech to vomit into the wound, which isn't great for a number of reasons. The best thing to do is to nick your fingernail under the sucker at the front and try to lever it off, do the same for the posterior sucker, then flick it away.

▼ The leech, a rather sophisticated member of the Annelid family.

"I'm rather partial to a good drop of Claret."

Leeches Conquer the French

Of course it is not all that fun standing in a pond in the middle of winter while sophisticated earthworms drain your blood. What's more, leeches can even kill. Napoleon's army in the Sinai drank from whatever source they could. The leeches they swallowed swelled and closed up the parts the Frenchmen liked to breathe through, which proved rather detrimental to their wellbeing.

Possibly the greatest use of leeches can be found in the rather marvelously named Tempest Prognosticator—a remarkable device for predicting stormy weather by Dr. George Merryweather. Leeches move to high ground when they sense a storm is coming, and so the rather ingenious Dr. Merryweather decided to use this behavior to give warning of impending "tempests." The leeches, or as Merryweather liked to call them, his "jury of philosophical councillors," attached to a tiny chain, crawled up to the top of a glass jar and tipped a lever to ring a bell, making everyone aware of the approaching storm. All in all we at The Proceedings rather like this slippery customer, and while he might stretch the definition of liking a Bloody Mary a bit far, our band of rag-tag scholars likes to think the leech gives rather more than it takes away.

A Farming leeches with your bare legs—without doubt one of the worst jobs in history.

V Leeches are found all over the place, even in the Antarctic.

25

BLUE-TAILED DAMSELFLY

ISCHNURA ELEGANS

The damselflies are members of the Odonata family, or literally the toothed jaws. Toothed in jaw they are for a very good reason because these are the "birds of prey" of the insect world—iridescent armored biplanes that pluck bugs from the heavens. They may be what make baby greenflies wake up in a sweat at night but, as their name suggests, they might be rather less macho than you'd think.

◀ This is a terrifying clanking machine of death, especially to small insects, and even more so for small insects that call him names.

So why put such insect-botherers in this marvelous menagerie? Well it seems that the male blue-tailed damselfly exhibits some rather unusual behavior if left to its own devices. If all ladies are removed from the males' abode, instead of retiring to the drawing room to talk cricket and affairs of state, they will start trying to court each other. Remarkably, they will do little dances for the other chaps in a bid to see if they can find a potential suitor, though the rather shortsighted researchers investigating this phenomenon did not think to drop in miniature bits of furniture and haberdashery to see if the gents would start making the place look nice.

Not surprisingly there is a sound biological reason for this same-sex behavior. The female damselflies come in a variety of colors and they only need to mate once in their life. They are

Fact

Same-sex behavior is rife in the animal kingdom. In fact, it is fair to say that no species has been found in which homosexual behavior definitely does not exist.

rather frigid and will go to great lengths to avoid being harassed by hordes of eager males, preferring instead to spend their days chomping on insects and whatnot. To avoid unwanted attention, some of the females simply look a bit more like their male counterparts. So there it is! A male damselfly that can be made to act like a dame because the dame can act like a chap! Huzzah!

(LEXICON)

Odonata

The garden-variety dragonfly is slightly chunkier than the damselfly, though a better way of telling these two death machines apart is that the damselfly keeps her wings flat and folded in to her body when she's at rest, while the dragonfly has her wings stuck out like an airplane.

Boys Will Be Girls

Of course, it would be ridiculous to compare this "situational homosexuality" in humans to the homoerotic damselfly dances. Thankfully, we are rather ridiculous down here at The Proceedings and we try to act silly at the first available opportunity. You see, even the toughest of tough guys can be taken in by this behavior. Don't believe me? Well take an example from Colditz Castle, the most famous Nazi prisoner-of-war camp in World War Two. The tales of derring-do and escape from Colditz are of course renowned, but there is a short tale that is less often told. To pass the time of day the inmates would stage plays, the cast of which would often include a dame. A rather feminine young soldier with a beautiful singing voice, who with respect will go unnamed, was selected for the role in the first play. That same young officer went on to play the lead female in subsequent plays, and slowly many of the inmates developed a crush on him. Before long they were showering him with gifts, holding open doors for him, and doffing their caps, in a most gentlemanly fashion.

"HANG ON A BLEEDING MINUTE, YOU'RE ARTHUR NOT MARTHA!"

▼ Blue-tailed damselflies are found in alternative bars around the European continent, and even in Britain.

DEATHSTALKER

LEIURUS QUINQUESTRIATUS

Scorpions kill ten times the number of people that snakes do, but thankfully the deathstalker isn't like the others. He likes kittens and always recycles and ... not really—he is the deadliest of the lot of them.

As if spiders weren't enough to make your good lady swoon, some decided to add a big, stingy harbinger of death on to their back. They are found pretty much everywhere below the Isle of Sheppey in Kent, England. I know, scorpions in Blighty, such an unlikely place to find the little monsters! They live pretty much everywhere south of the line of latitude 49° north, bar Antarctica and New Zealand.

Most stings from scorpions have little more potency than a bee sting. Of the two thousand or so species of scorpion, only about fifty produce a poison potent enough to be considered dangerous. Of these fifty only half can produce it in sufficient quantities to pose a lethal risk to humans. Still, there are many deaths by scorpion sting around

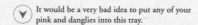

It would be a very bad idea to put any of your pink and danglies into this tray.

The deathstalker can be avoided by not going to various sandy bits of North Africa and the Arab peninsula.

the world each year, and three quarters of these deaths can be attributed to just two types of scorpion: the fat-tailed scorpion and of course our chum the deathstalker.

It comes down to the potency of the fellow's stinger juice, which is loaded with an array of neurotoxins and has a very low LD50. Toxicity is everywhere, and toxicologists give most things an LD50 number, namely the lethal dose for 50% of a given population. So for example, sugar has an LD50 of 0.45 oz per lb (30g/kg), so for an average man of about 165 lb (75 kg), about 5 lb (2.25 kg) of sugar taken orally will not only make a very sweet cup of tea, it will very likely kill him.

What's Your Poison?

About 7 oz (200 g) of salt will kill you, while about ½ oz (13 g) of caffeine will not only wake you up, but will put you to sleep rather quickly too. Botulinum toxin is the most toxic thing on the planet with an LD50 of about 0.000075 mg (a minute amount), and is, surprisingly, the stuff that aging starlets inject into their faces to keep their skin looking young. Sadly we cannot give you an LD50 for the deathstalker; as we mentioned, he hedges his bets by injecting you with an array of nasties. Learned types are now using these toxins to treat a number of illnesses, including brain tumors and diabetes. So there it is; he may not do his recycling or have a love of kittens, but he does save lives. The deathstalker: the deadliest lifesaver there ever was.

Mating (or making sweet music) with a partner as gruesome as a scorpion is going to be quite a challenge. Once the prospective partners have established that they aren't going to eat each other, the male grabs the female's claws and they begin a little dance called the Promenade à Deux. It sounds quite romantic, I know, but I assure you it is hardly a candlelit table for two at the Ritz. The male is in fact dragging her around trying to find a suitable spot to place a packet of sperm on the ground. Once he's put his seed down, he pulls her over the top of it to inseminate her, at which point they each realize they are having a romantic liaison with one of the most dangerous creatures on the planet and make a break for it. Interestingly, and unlike most arachnids, the scorpions are viviparous, meaning they give birth to live young. The average litter of about eight scorplings will travel around on their mother's back for the first few weeks of their lives.

LEOPARD SLUG

LIMAX MAXIMUS

Meet the positively peachy leopard slug, or Limax maximus, *which means "Great Slug!" These nocturnal spotty slimers can grow as large as your forearm, which makes them one of the largest land slugs in the world. Though it is not their size that gets these slugs into this book, oh no. You see, it turns out that the leopard slug has a sex life that would make rabbits blush.*

Nuptial naughtiness can wait, dear reader, as there are many other curiosities about this marvelous slug. Of course slugs don't have a shell, or at least not one that is visible—many slugs have them hidden away in their body as a vestigial structure from their evolutionary past. As Darwin exquisitely put it, "Rudimentary organs may be compared with the letters in a word, still retained in the spelling, but become useless in the pronunciation." Why would the slug want to forgo its shell? Well, put simply, shells are cumbersome and not entirely necessary; slugs can move around underground when the weather isn't to their liking, whereas snails have taken a different strategy and simply curl up in their houses to hide. This great slug doesn't get into The Proceedings because he is a rather nifty mover, either, even though he can zip around about three times faster than your average slug. He needs to, as he is not a big fan of salads and much prefers to gobble up other, slower slugs.

This slimy fellow may be strange for many reasons, but there is one reason he has caused a right hullabaloo down at The Proceedings. Yes, it's time for the bit about hanky-panky. Their night of debauchery begins as they circle around each

> **LEXICON**
>
> ## Apophallation
>
> The act of chewing off a partner's penis is thankfully rarely practiced by creatures other than slugs.

The leopard slug has what can only be described as the most depraved sex life of the animal kingdom, not least because he will try to eat your wedding tackle at the end of it.

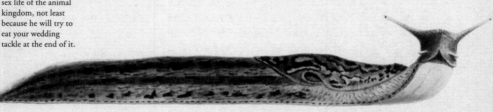

"FANCY GOING OUT FOR A BITE TO EAT?"

Leopard slugs are available in a variety of colors, though it is unwise to go on a date with any of them.

These great slugs were originally found in these parts of Europe. You'll be pleased to hear that you can now find them farther afield, including the Americas.

LEXICON

Slugs and snails

Snails have shells, whereas slugs don't, right? Well, surprisingly, many slugs have the evolutionary remnants of a tiny shell in their bodies. Such defunct structures are known as vestigial structures (see p. 105), much like the human appendix.

The vermiform appendix, AKA the wiggly wormy thing at the bottom of the cecum illustrated here, is a vestigial structure in humans with no known use. Charles Darwin wrote that it is perhaps the remains of an old stomach that our ancestors used to digest leaves.

other, slobbering all over their respective partner. After the hours of licky foreplay, the rather adventurous couple climb up a tree and entwine around each other before lowering themselves down on a mucus string. Once suspended in mid-air and spinning around, a huge penis comes out of each of their heads and each of these tangles around the other. The penises fan out into a rather smashing flower-like structure, at which point they exchange sperm. Sometimes the penises will become so entangled that things really do get to the worst possible scenario—one will chew off the other's penis. The newly neutered slug will still be able to mate, but only as a lady, although thankfully it doesn't often come to this. This rather eventful night is ended when the two slugs drop down to the floor and slither away into the night to lay thousands of eggs. How romantic.

So there he is: *Limax maximus* ... what a really great slug!

MAGICICADA

MAGICICADA SPP.

Meet the magicicada, so called because she is a magic cicada. Don't worry, she isn't going to bore us to tears by sawing some girl in half, nor is she about to pull a bunny from her hat, though she may well just appear out of thin air.

Cicadas are a type of insect that are famous for making a loud din, and so are often mistakenly lumped in with the crickets and grasshoppers. Probably because they are such noisy buggers, a group of cicadas sound like grasshoppers but there can be so many of them they can be as loud as a rock concert. While there are about 2,500 species of cicada, only a few of them are considered magical. These magicicadas are larval for most of their life, living in the soil as tiny nymphs far away from anything that might think them tasty. Once every 13 or 17 years, however, they suddenly decide *en masse* that they are sick of living under the ground.

"There is nothing up my left sleeve."

On this magical spring evening, the teenage magicicadas bundle out. As they sing their mating song, the sheer number of them produces such a hullabaloo that they can be heard from miles around. The females are fertilized, they lay their eggs, and then they die—all within a week or two. The eggs of course develop into larvae, which wait underground for another 13 or 17 years until they all emerge *en masse* again. Magic!

Magicicadas perform their infrequent magic acts in the northeastern part of North America.

LEXICON

Predator satiation

So why all this impeccably timed fornication? Well, emerging all together is a form of collective defense against predators. If they came out willy-nilly every year over a long period of time they would quite probably meet a load of chubby predators who could snaffle them without a second thought. The magicicadas do meet predators, lots of them—reptiles, birds, squirrels, and many more—and the greedy buggers have their fill, but because they emerge all at once it just isn't possible to eat every single magicicada.

BLISTER BEETLE

FAMILY: MELOIDAE

Beetles are the most numerous species on the planet—incredibly, about a quarter of all the known animal species on the big wet rock we call home are beetles. In fact one in four living things is a beetle. There are millions of them. You could fill the biggest stadium in the world with beetles, hundreds of times over, although this would prove nothing and would result in a bloody awful mess and some rather miffed football fans.

The blister beetle is a smashing example of our rather numerous chums. It is so called because it secretes a noxious liquid that causes blisters. One species of blister beetle is the famed Spanish fly, which is neither Spanish nor a fly, though it is famed for its ability to cause the male member to swell—a property that increases its value in the eyes of many. Unfortunately, it is rather painful too; the blistering effect of the beetle causes irritation of the urethra and leads to priapism (a constant stiffy).

It is important to mention that the chemical is rather poisonous, and has been used to knock off a number of famous figures throughout history. Not only is it a rather dreadful way to kick the bucket, it is an embarrassing one too.

A Blister beetles have a worldwide distribution, though not all of them will cause pant-tumescence.

> It is a very bad idea to eat this chap; for starters he won't appreciate it.

LEXICON

Brood parasites

The blister beetle larvae are gruesome little sods. They form into a bee-sized ball, add a squirt of the bee's favorite perfume, and wait for Mr. Bee to join the party, at which point the larvae attach to him and hitch a ride back to the nest where they gobble up all the nice food that was meant for the little bees.

"No, no, don't mind them ... right, who's up for nuptials?"

NEW ZEALAND BATFLY

MYSTACINOBIA ZEALANDICA

Sometimes we question whether the gift of flight is such a great advantage. Apart from the fact that it's a tad strenuous, what really is the point in taking flight if there are no predators on the ground to gobble you up? All that zooming around may be rather good fun but it takes up far too much energy, so why not have a stroll around the forest floor instead, in the manner of those adorable, tubby, feathered lumps the kakapos (pp. 124–5) and kiwis?

A number of creatures have given up on the whole flying idea in New Zealand—a phenomenon specific to a country where there are no indigenous mammals. While some creatures have given up on flying, others are still able to but don't. It's more that they've given up on all that strenuous eating "on the fly" business. So when the sun dips into the Pacific after a long hard day, the New Zealand lesser short-tailed bat, or the *pekapeka* as the natives call it, flies out into the inky nightness. He is not flailing around in the inky nightness for long, though. To find food he drops to the forest floor and shuffles around, eating up all the nice creepy-crawlies and whatnot.

It'll Never Fly

Remarkable stuff, we are sure you'll agree! Although we are not here to chat about the incredible New Zealand lesser short-tailed bat; we're here to talk about the New Zealand batfly, or *Mystacinobia zealandica* for short. The batfly lives happily with the bats in the north of New Zealand where they hide away together in the hollows of old trees. Incredibly, these flies have given up on the whole idea of flying, preferring instead to sit around lazily eating the guano that the bats produce. As well as being served up a huge excess of delicious grub (if festering bat poop is your idea of deli-

This splendid fly has given up on the flying-through-the-air nonsense and settled down to a more social existence. Delightful.

> The forests along the northern tip of New Zealand—a place where batfly and bat live rather happily.

cious grub), they spend their time doing other things, like socializing. Although they haven't quite mastered bridge yet, they do have little soirées, handing out bat poop on blini and generally getting to know each other better. They like to clean and groom one another, which strikes me as rather sensible behavior if you live on bat poop.

The batflies have begun to evolve into something rather more un-fly-like than the little fellows they descended from. Indeed, there is nothing more un-fly-like than a fly that doesn't fly. They have organized themselves into something resembling a caste system, much like ants (pp. 39 & 54–5), termites (p. 23), and naked mole rats (pp. 148–9). There are batflies that tend to the young, and guards who protect the colony. So there we have it: the bat that has given up flying has a fly that has given up flying to become something more than a fly ... or something like that.

(LEXICON)

Caste systems

The evolution of so-called "caste systems"—or eusociality (see p. 149), as learned types like to call it—is worthy of special mention. A caste system is quite simply a division of labor in a group of animals. Often there will be a reproductive queen and some workers and soldiers who are rather indifferent to carnal pleasures. For Darwin, explaining how such systems may have evolved was his "one special problem," although nowadays we think we may well have worked it out. It has been observed that animals will lay down their own lives for kin that share the same genetic material as them, a prime example of which is eusocial behavior. Blood is indeed thicker than water.

> You can bat an eye at the New Zealand batfly on the northern tip of New Zealand.

NAMIBIAN FOG-BASKING BEETLE

ONYMACRIS UNGUICULARIS

———⚬———

On a foggy morning you can find old Onymacris unguicularis *standing on its head on top of a sand dune with its bottom in the air. No, the fellow hasn't been drinking all night. Quite the opposite in fact: he's absolutely parched.*

Water, lovely stuff, wash with it, make tea with it ... life started in it and took quite some time to get out of it. I know how it feels—it is difficult getting out of the tub at times. Our friends the Namibian fog-basking beetles are equally fond of the stuff. The local bushmen refer to them as the *tok-tokkie* beetle because they attract a mate by tapping the ground with their bottoms to make a noise. It is not the rectal Morse code chat-up lines, though, that makes this chap so splendid. The fog-basking beetle has developed a rather nifty way of getting a drink. As a morning fog rolls in from the sea, the beetle goes to meet it, pointing his *derrière* up to the sky. His carapace, which is made up of a series of hydrophobic peaks and troughs, is so magnificently evolved that it allows the fog to settle on it. The water rolls off each trough and begins to form droplets, which then naturally run down the inverted beetle's body and into his mouth. Smashing, isn't it?

Fact

The fog-basking beetle's marvelous carapace gave a group of military engineers a quite splendid idea. You see, they made a series of fabrics using glass beads and waxy coatings and used them to create huge and inexpensive fog catchers, so that parched locals in dry places can get a glass of water.

"Blasted weather. I forgot my umbrella too."

The Namibian fog-basking beetle is found in the Namib desert and may or may not be basking in fog.

Water

The wet stuff is flabbergasting in its epic grandeur, forming lakes of incomprehensible dimensions, and huge rivers that course through the land, slicing through granite mountains like an unimaginably slow paring knife. The oceans are so massive that we haven't got the foggiest what lurks at the bottom of them. Water blankets the planet, our blue Earth, covering two-thirds of it. All the more reason then to be surprised by the fact that there is hardly a drop of the stuff. You don't believe me? Take a look:

Told you. Yes really, that's it; that tiny blue droplet is all the lakes, all the rivers, all the puddles, all the seas, all the ice, and all that we have. Thankfully, we don't treat it too badly. Actually, all this talk of water, one is going to need to go for a quick ... oh dear lordy, what are we doing?

Water is essential to all known forms of life; it allows all sorts of curious things to go on in it and it allows itself to be manipulated in all manner of ways. Which is awfully sporting of it considering that life seems dependent on water's

solvent and chemical properties. It is also kind enough to float when it freezes, which doesn't sound like much until you realize that if it sank it would very likely turn the planet into a rather large ice ball.

It turns out that water's rather felicitous properties are important not just for the Earth, as we have certainly detected water on other planets. Indeed there is likely to be an awful lot more in the universe, as water's two components, hydrogen and oxygen, are the most common elements there are. All good news, then, that there is water on other planets and that extra-terrestrial life is perhaps inevitable.

While governments nowadays are happy to kick the hell out of some poor bloody country for the sake of oil, the looming population crisis means the next wars will be fought over a far more valuable fluid resource. Actually, I think I will have that drink after all.

◄ Over the last 40 years, the Aral Sea in Central Asia has shrunk to ten percent of its original size.

BONE-EATING SNOT FLOWER

OSEDAX MUCOFLORIS

This is not the sort of bloom that will win you the favor of a girlfriend,
we can assure you. The bone-eating snot flower is not a flower at all but is in fact
a fine example of a zombie worm. These worms haven't earned their zombie moniker
thanks to a slow yet persistent shambling gait, nor for their penchant for a brain terrine.
They do, however, like to feast on the dead.

Fact

Only discovered in the last ten years, six species of zombie worm have now been named, although it is thought that many more must have become extinct when the whale populations were decimated by as much as 90 percent at the back end of the nineteenth century.

"Whale fall" is a bit like "rainfall," it just hurts more. When a whale dies it sinks to the bottom of the ocean where it provides a plethora of beasties with quite a banquet. These carcasses dot the ocean floor, providing oases for the deep-water creatures that live there. All manner of meat-eaters take their place at the table: crabs, squat lobsters, sleeper sharks, and the particularly delightful hagfish (pp. 80–1). A hideous cacophony it is too—if you do ever get an invite, I would implore you not even to send back the RSVP. Once the whale's bones are stripped of flesh, it is time for the zombie worms to move in. They set roots into the bones, like ghoulish flowers, cracking the outer casing to get at the fatty marrow beneath and gorging themselves on the sweet insides.

The bone-eating snot flower reproduces constantly, with the female keeping a harem of males inside her tubes so that her eggs can be constantly fertilized. The eggs are cast into the oceanic currents, hopefully to find another whale carcass that has been stripped down, rather like a zombie dandelion clock. Though by now I'm sure you agree dear reader, the last bouquet you want to bestow on your girlfriend is a bone-eating snot flower.

The bone-eating snot flower is not a flower at all, though it does look as though it has come from the nose of a hay-fever sufferer.

The bone-eating snot flower was recently discovered in the North Sea, but it may well have a worldwide distribution.

BULLET ANT

PARAPONERA CLAVATA

The bullet ant is so named because the power of its sting is said to be as painful as having a lump of searing hot lead, traveling at a couple of hundred miles an hour, leave the end of a rifle for a very important meeting with your buttocks. The truly awful news is that the name is justified.

The fact that it possesses the most painful sting in the world according to the Schmidt sting pain index (see p. 41) is fine testament to what a brute this ant is. Just one sting can cause nausea, sweating, numbness, swearing, and general uproar. It is fair to say that the sting of the bullet ant really, really hurts. It can also bite so hard that if it doesn't break whatever it bites, the force of its jaws will catapult the little bugger up into the air. The Satere-Mawe people of Brazil use these formidable foes as an initiation into manhood. They take the ants, put them to sleep with a natural chloroform, then weave them into gloves, with the stinger facing inwards. With only a bit of charcoal to protect them, the pain endured by the young lads is naturally excruciating and lasts for quite some time. Thankfully, the hapless Satere-Mawe boys only have to go through the initiation an agonizing 20 times, without putting up too much of a fuss.

It is fair to say that wearing gloves made of hundreds of creatures that give you the feeling you've just been shot probably hurts. It also goes some of the way to explaining why teenage Satere-Mawe are sullen and covered in red spots.

Fact

One of the only enemies of the bullet ant, apart from those weird big bald apes who inexplicably sew them into warm-weather attire, is a fungus. The Cordyceps *fungus gets into the bodies of the little terrors and pops a mushroom out of the top of its head, killing the ant in the process.*

"You should meet my friend 'The Chainsaw Hamster.'"

If you don't like suffering a bite that feels like you've taken a hit from a blunderbuss, don't go here.

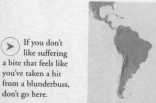

TARANTULA HAWK

PEPSIS SPP.

The tarantula: a big, ugly, eight-legged bitey bastard ... not ideal babysitting material in anyone's book. Oddly, the extraordinary tarantula hawk likes to leave junior with this evil terror. Still, she does take the precaution of paralyzing the bugger first, which is a bit like leaving sherry with the nanny.

Tarantula hawks are actually a type of wasp, although a frighteningly big one as you would expect. They possess an incredibly powerful sting: according to the Schmidt sting index it is second in painfulness only to the bullet ant—affording its unhappy victim a dose of pain that is "blinding, fierce, shockingly electric. [Like a] running hair drier has been dropped into your bubble bath." Which sounds like one to be avoided. The tarantula hawk seeks out a tarantula and will unbelievably get into a quick tussle with the swine, before dealing a knockout blow to paralyze it. No one is really sure how this happens, but it is probably that this flying assassin is using some sort of pheromone. Most zoologists, being human, tend to avoid having to handle them and will go to great lengths to avoid publishing papers on "How the stingiest stinger you couldn't even imagine interacts with the spider from Hades," presumably preferring to write papers on "Who prefers snuggles most: penguins, otters, or puppies?"

Once the tarantula is paralyzed, the wasp then crawls over it, checking it is exactly the right species.

> ### LEXICON
>
> ## Parasitoids
>
> Parasitoids live for a good while on or inside a rather unlucky host animal, a lot like a parasite. Unluckier still for the host, the difference between a parasitoid and a parasite is that the former will definitely kill them.

"MRS. TARANTULA HAWK WAS A SUCKER FOR A BEAUTIFUL BOUQUET."

▼ Tarantula hawks are found only in the Americas, much to the relief of tarantulas around the rest of the globe.

◀ While the young dine on tarantulas, adults slurp the sweet nectar of flowers.

The annual spider and wasp tea dance was always a charming night.

When the wasp is satisfied, he delivers a potent neurotoxin, drags it to the bottom of his burrow, lays a single egg on its body, and seals up the burrow with the spider still comatose inside. Eventually the larva hatches and sticks its mouth into the tarantula's abdomen to suck the spider dry. When the squishy bits are gone, the rapidly growing larva moves on to the still alive, and still fresh, essential organs. The spider of course dies, as it really could have used those essential organs to live, which is why they were bloody well called essential in the first place. With the buffet slain, the wasp larva builds a cocoon to metamorphose ... into another tarantula-molesting machine. Quite delightful!

Surprisingly, after they've grown up, these rather devilish characters don't eat tarantulas anymore. They are actually nectarivorous, meaning they eat the sweet sugary ambrosia of flowers and are said to be partial to a bit of boozy fermenting fruit. It is a wise man, or indeed tarantula, that avoids a very, very drunk tarantula hawk.

The Schmidt Sting Pain Index

Justin O. Schmidt is a legendary entomologist who took it upon himself to be bothered by just about every member of the Hymenoptera—that's bees, wasps, and ants to lesser mortals—and recorded just how painful each one was in his Schmidt sting pain index.

 # 1.0 Sweat bee: *Light, ephemeral, almost fruity. A tiny spark has singed a single hair on your arm.*

 # 1.2 Fire ant: *Sharp, sudden, mildly alarming. Like walking across a shag carpet & reaching for the light switch.*

 # 1.8 Bullhorn acacia ant: *A rare, piercing, elevated sort of pain. Someone has fired a staple into your cheek.*

 # 2.0 Bald-faced hornet: *Rich, hearty, slightly crunchy. Similar to getting your hand mashed in a revolving door.*

 # 2.0 Yellowjacket: *Hot and smoky, almost irreverent. Imagine W. C. Fields extinguishing a cigar on your tongue.*

 # 2.0 Honey bee and European hornet: *Like a matchhead that flips off and burns on your skin.*

 # 3.0 Red harvester ant: *Bold and unrelenting. Somebody is using a drill to excavate your ingrown toenail.*

 # 3.0 Paper wasp: *Caustic and burning. Distinctly bitter aftertaste. Like spilling a beaker of hydrochloric acid on a paper cut.*

 # 4.0 Pepsis wasp: *Blinding, fierce, shockingly electric. A running hair drier has been dropped into your bubble bath.*

 # 4.0+ Bullet ant: *Pure, intense, brilliant pain. Like fire-walking over flaming charcoal with a 3-inch rusty nail in your heel.*

VELVET WORM

PHYLUM: ONYCHOPHORA

This fabulously decadent dame is the velvet worm, so named because his downy skin is as plush and perverse as a fine Venetian velvet. It is not for his opulent appearance, nor for his sartorial elegance, however, that this creature glides his way into this bestiary. It is rather for reasons of some exquisitely unusual hunting habits.

Fact

In 1909, a marvelous fellow by the name of Charles Walcott took some time off from his preferred pastime of doing amazing things, and instead found something amazing, namely a number of fossils. Even though the fossils were really rather special, Charles would never know just how special these soft-bodied specimens would become. While they were variously placed in known groups of animals—a jellyfish here, a worm there—it turns out that they were not just species gone extinct but entire types of animals we had lost to time. Thankfully at least one of these incredibly bizarre creatures has relatives in the present-day—it turns out the rather surreal specimen aptly called Hallucigenia *was a velvet worm.*

There the velvet worm goes, sashaying his way through the forest like a rather leggy worm in a smoking jacket, and all the while looking for victims by quite literally sniffing them out. When he finds some unwitting victim to terrorize, he rears up and squirts sticky goo everywhere like a primordial Spiderman. The victim is stuck fast by the sticky threads, leaving the dastardly velvet worm to inject his prey with poisonous saliva and entrail-liquefying enzymes. He then chomps on a suitable spot and sucks the gooey insides out—wonderful! After this fine brunch, he spends a good bit of time chomping up all his sticky stuff to use on some other hapless victim.

This rather spider-like way of eating is not an accident. Although originally scientists thought the velvet worm was a type of earthworm, it seems that this rakish fellow is actually a lot more closely related

The velvet worm lives on leaf mold. Of course, she's had someone in to make the place look fabulous.

Between 1910 and 1924, Charles Doolittle Walcott collected 65,000 specimens from the Burgess Shale, often referred to as "the most important fossils of all time."

"IF YOU'LL JUST FOLLOW ME TO THE DRAWING ROOM."

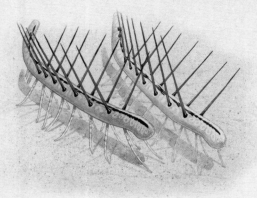

LEXICON

Viviparity

There are a number of different ways for an animal to give birth. Viviparous, whereby the young animal develops inside mom, as in humans. Oviparous, in which the animal develops inside an egg, like in the chickens or echidna. Ovoviviparous, whereby junior develops inside an egg, inside mom. The majority of velvet worms favor this method, although there are species that are oviparous and others that are viviparous.

"PEOPLE CAN BE SO UNKIND."

When *Hallucigenia,* along with its incredible fossil bedfellows, were found, the esteemed audience gave a rather unusual response: they laughed.

to Arachnids. Some learned types have proposed that way back in the depths of time the velvet worms were the closest shared relative of the nematode worms and spiders—indeed they have characteristics of both. Evolutionary conjecture aside, there is a most obscene additional oddity that one can't fail to mention. As you will know by now, we at The Proceedings have a predilection for the somewhat obscene, and on that front the velvet worm does not disappoint. She has, you see, rather peculiar mating habits.

Once the chap, who is much smaller than the ladies, has found an eager mate, he deposits his sperm in a sac and leaves it on the female's back—somewhat raffish behavior admittedly. The number of sacs on the females back can increase over time, and there are often many of these spermatophores from different males all over her, after which the packages are absorbed into her side. The sperm swim willy-nilly through her blood until they reach the sperm-storage organs, whereupon she is fertilized.

These aren't the only odd baby-making behaviors velvet worms display, however, as some species lay eggs, others hatch eggs inside their bodies, and some actually have live young.

The velvet worms follow a peculiar distribution, at least until you look at how the world was compressed together a long time ago, which hints at just how long they have been on the planet.

PORTUGUESE MAN O' WAR

PHYSALIA PHYSALIS

———❦———

There is something really rather surprising about this creature, or should we say creatures. You see, it is not a creature at all, but a collection of different animals, all pretty much useless on their own but highly effective when they work together. A little like dwarves in a raincoat; if, of course, dwarves standing on each other's shoulders added up to be a big death machine rather than a slightly comical tall man.

There are four different types of creature that go into making a man o' war, and it is said that there was quite an argument when they were trying to decide what to look like. In the end they agreed to look like a caravel, an ancient ship with triangular sails, otherwise known as the Portuguese man o' war. Each creature that goes into

"OH YES, AFTER ALL THESE YEARS WE STILL GET ALONG FABULOUSLY. WE FIND COMMUNICATION IS THE KEY."

◄ The blue coloration of the Portuguese man o' war has earned it a number of different monikers, including "blue bottle" and "blue bubble."

▼ The Portuguese man o' war can be found as far north as the Hebrides and as far south as New Zealand.

Though Ernst Haeckel was a respected naturalist and talented artist, his subjects were often annoyed that the final portrait "didn't really look like me."

making this rather remarkable fellow is an incredibly specialized medusa or polyp, so specialized in fact that they are quite useless without each other. I like to think of them as a gin and tonic, with ice and a slice—all largely forgettable on their own, but something really rather magical when mixed together. The different parts of the man o' war get along fabulously too—there are the bladder creatures that make the sail, the stingy buggers who catch and haul the prey, the stomach animals that digest the fishy treats, and the breeding creatures whose job it is to make sure there are junior man o' wars causing havoc in other parts of the world.

As it is not a single creature, the man o' war isn't a jellyfish: It is actually a siphonophore. What's more, their convivial nature is not just reserved for each other, as these animal hodgepodges get along with other colonies rather well too, forming swarms in the thousands. Each single colony can have a trail that sweeps through the ocean for 165 feet (50 m), and these trails are laced with deadly blastocysts: stinging cells that are neurotoxic, paralyzing fish within seconds, and sometimes killing humans. The blastocysts work by firing when the hair at the top of the cell is brushed, shooting out at an acceleration of 40,000 G. That's really rather fast, by the way—the maximum G in a fighter jet turning is between 9 and 12. So if you do see these blue blobs coming towards you it may be best you get out of their way, every single last one of them.

LEXICON

Man of War

The man of war was a ship dating back to the 16th century that was quite simply not to be trifled with. In fact they were said to be the most powerful of the time. They were based on the caravel, a Portuguese ship that was built for speed and agility and was used as an exploration vessel in the Age of Discovery.

WATER BEAR

PHYLUM: TARDIGRADA

Water bears, also known as the tardigrades or moss piglets, are everywhere, from the top of the highest mountains to the depths of the deepest abyss. Some of our more savvy readers will have quite rightly surmised (because they haven't seen them at the village tea parties with a slice of Victoria sponge cake) that water bears are very, very small. They are also really rather adorable.

The water bear is so called for his ursine good looks and waddling gait, rather like a chubby grizzly plumped up on salmon for winter. A thousand species of tardigrade have been named and undoubtedly many more are yet to be identified. There can be as many as 250,000 of them in a liter of swamp water. However, omnipresence, cuteness, and looking like a bear are not enough to propel a critter into this book—there is more to this fellow than meets the eye. You see, this chap is in fact the toughest creature on the planet, tougher even than the honey badger (pp. 154–5), though a lot less handy in a ruckus.

These miniature water bears can take any punishment to be honest, including temperatures as low as –460 degrees Fahrenheit (–273ºC), which is about as close to cold as you can get, if that makes any sense.

> Don't let the water bear's waddling demeanor fool you, this is one tough little customer.

*"THAT'S RICH COMING FROM YOU
'HOUSE MONKEY.' "*

Fact

They can survive temperatures hotter than a boiling kettle, up to an incredible 300 degrees Fahrenheit (151 °C) and can live for a decade without a drink, though why the blazes they would want to do that is anyone's guess. What's more, they can even survive far too much of the wet stuff, withstanding about six thousand atmospheres of pressure. In other words, they could live in water six times deeper than the deepest ocean trench. Tardigrades can easily put up with about one thousand times the dose of radiation that would take out a human, and happily waddle off. They have even spent ten days shoved out of a space shuttle window, and of course they thought that the whole trip was just dandy. Calling them names like "fat little multi-legged bear thing" doesn't even hurt them.

The key to this rather remarkable resilience is that they can basically die and resurrect themselves. When things are looking tough they will simply shut down their metabolism. Water bears will stop every single bodily process, including repair, reproduction, and development. Then when everything looks peachy once again, they'll wake up, have a bit of a yawn and a stretch, and waddle off. For this reason, although they are tough as old boots, they are pretty much useless when it comes to fisticuffs.

LEXICON

Panspermia

As we mentioned, possibly the harshest environment to live in is outer space: blistering radiation, a complete lack of oxygen, frightfully chilly, and not a decent bistro for miles. Naturally the teeny water bear takes all this in his rather short stride. Though he may well not be the only one ... indeed it may have been one of these tiny space travelers that brought life to our planet. The panspermia theory—the idea that life came from another planet—was first put forward by Greek philosopher Anaxagoras in the fifth century BC. Recently, and rather tantalizingly, spacecraft have intercepted comets containing many organic compounds in them, compounds that without a shadow of a doubt did not come from Earth.

Life is bloody tough. The toughest of the tough bits of life are known as the extremophiles. They are found in superheated volcanic geysers and oil wells, in nuclear power stations and polar ice, in the middle of rocks four miles (6.4 km) beneath the Earth's surface, and in the driest deserts on the Earth. Life is even found in thermal vents hotter than boiling water in the deepest abyss of the ocean, and even, inexplicably, in cans of hairspray. Needless to say, not many things can call themselves extremophiles. Even fewer ultra-tough individuals get to call themselves polyextremophiles. No, it is not a female extremophile, nor a parrot extremophile for that matter. The polyextremophiles can take a number of these unbelievably harsh conditions, and unsurprisingly the water bear is included in this rather tough bunch.

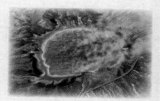

(A) The colored rings from this piping-hot pool are in fact extremophiles.

(◄) The water bears can be found everywhere: from pole to pole and from the top of Mount Everest to the bottom of the Marianas trench.

ZOMBIE FLY

PSEUDACTEON SPP.

These tiny, tiny flies are actually gruesome killing machines. What is more, they WANT TO EAT YOUR BRAINS—well, they do if you happen to be a type of South American ant, which I grant is unlikely as you would probably be reading a Spanish or Quechuan A Beastly Menagerie or some such, and you would probably have difficulty with the pages. Actually, that would be the least of your problems if you had an ant-decapitating fly on your hands.

"BRRRRAAAAAAIIIIIIINNNNNNNNSSS!"

These zombie flies come from a diverse bunch of flies known as the scuttle flies—so called because, yes quite, you've seen them scuttling around. What these ant-decapitating scuttle flies do is jump on the back of some hapless ant, stab it with their ovipositor, and stick an egg into the poor sod. The egg quickly develops into a larva and wriggles up the body and into the head. There the hungry maggot chows down on the brain until it is entirely gobbled up. Remarkably, the ant—while having to take a bit more time over the *Times* crossword these days—is still able to walk and do other menial chores. Of course, if this were done to you or me, we would a) be very unhappy about it, and b) be quite dead, and therefore probably would not have minded it that much. Ants, however, have a number of ganglia down their backs that act much like miniature brains.

After the ant-decapitating fly larva has been shuffling around in the ant's head for about two weeks, having a merry old time enjoying the view and the cuisine, she releases an enzyme that dissolves the muscles in the back of the ant's head. The ant's head pops off, leaving the larva to have a bit of a snooze, pupating to work off the delicious lunch

Fact

Though they sound like a gruesome bunch, the ant-decapitating zombie flies are actually on our side. Invasive fire ants (pp. 54–5) are spreading across the globe, generally being a real nuisance, and displacing rare and native wildlife (for example, the Texas horned lizard, pp. 104–5). Our brain-eating chums are proving to be quite an ally in the fight against the invaders.

> After a number of weeks having its brain eaten, the ant's head drops off.

she's had. A couple of weeks later, and after a bit of a costume change, off she flies to go and harass some other poor unsuspecting victim.

The ant-decapitating flies are part of the rather diverse Phoridae family—a group containing the rather gruesome coffin flies that feast on the human remains inside coffins. They include the omnivorous species *Megaselia scalaris* that will happily eat virtually anything: plants, open wounds on any animal, living lung tissue, even boot polish and paint. Although it is the ant-decapitating zombie fly that we have in our hearts (though thankfully not in our heads), the ants that they attack no doubt keep them in a lower esteem. The lengths to which these ants go to avoid having their brain eaten are remarkable, and quite understandable. Some species of leaf-cutter ant have even gone as far as working in pairs: one to carry the leaf and one to tussle with the ant-decapitating flies.

"NOW IS NOT THE TIME TO LOSE YOUR HEAD."

The Megaselia scalaris—*or "coffin fly"—is a relative of the scuttle fly that likes its main course to be a bit more human. This tiny fly, less than ⅕ inch (5 mm) in length, scrabbles six feet under looking for human flesh to feast upon. These gruesome little terrors breed upon our dead so successfully they can live happily for generation after generation in a coffin. It is often said that when a body is exhumed, thousands of the tiny winged horrors come bursting forth. Incredible breeders they are, too; a single pair could feasibly make more than 55 million horrors in as little as 60 days.*

> Ant-decapitating flies are found anywhere there are ants. They'd be daft to go anywhere else.

> This dastardly looking thing is the ovipositor, the part that jabs an egg into the ant's body. Things really go downhill for the ant from this point on.

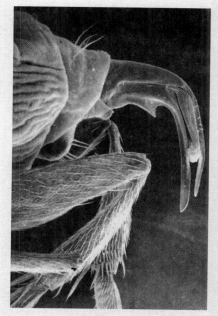

JUMPING SPIDERS

FAMILY: SALTICIDAE

Jumping spiders are a rather charming bunch. They are one of the most numerous types of arachnid, with about 5,000 species spanning the globe, although—fix yourself a Martini and read on, dear reader—they aren't a bit like your run-of-the-mill eight-legged spider.

These charming spiders don't really fit in with their peers, which of course can only endear them to our band of *bon vivants*. They are, put quite simply, not very spider-like. Instead of a terrifying lolloping blur of legs, beady little eyes, and venomous gnashers— attributes that can turn even the most ardent animal lover into a genocidal animapath—they are instead fluffy and doe-eyed and actually make you want to pick them up for a bit of a spidery snuggle.

This, sadly, would be quite impossible as they tend to be about ⅕ inch (5 mm) long, although they do try to compensate for this by behaving in a rather precious manner. If you presented your pinkie to another type of spider it would presumably either scamper over to try to give you a venomous bite, or to just watch you squeal like a girl—whichever is most terrifying. The jumping spider reacts quite differently, inquisitively wondering what the blazes the pink sausagey thing is and going over to investigate. They move not surprisingly in a jerky jumping manner, but amazingly they don't use muscles to haul their furry bodies around; their legs operate using a system of hydraulics. Like a mechanical digger, they utilize fluid (blood in the case of our adorable arachnid),

The jumping spiders make up 13% of all spider species. Unsurprisingly, they are rather widely distributed.

"FANCY A SNUGGLE?"

which they pump around their system. The fluid fills their hollow limbs, causing them to extend rapidly. This rather marvelous adaptation allows them to jump really rather high—up to 80 times their own height—without having to rely on enormous legs like grasshoppers and other jumpers.

You Pussycat!

The jumping spiders also have incredible eyesight; it is ten times better than that of the dragonflies, who are patrons of the best peepers by far in the six-legged insect kingdom. The furry bouncers use their remarkable vision to stalk their prey, rather than putting up big and quite frankly frightful webs everywhere. It did confuse learned types for some time as to exactly how something with such a tiny brain can use its eyes to hunt. Predatory mammals, such as cats and humans, have

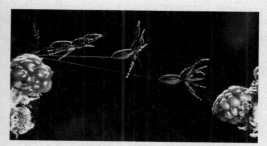

▼ Jumping spiders are, unsurprisingly, spiders that jump.

evolved incredibly complex and clever brains to deal with the amount of information our eyes bring in. The information is sifted and sorted so that we can take what we need from it without going stark-raving bonkers. The jumping spiders, it turns out, have evolved in a very different manner. While they can see perfectly well, they are able only to see a very small part of something at a time. If they were presented with a pigeon, they would not only be annoyed at your poor taste in presents, but they wouldn't be able to comprehend its magnitude. This is, incidentally, a philosophical argument as to why we cannot see our gods—they are just too enormous for our tiny minds to compute, though the likelihood that pigeons are deities in the eyes of jumping spiders is somewhat slim.

So give a wave hello to the rather delightful jumping spider—our fuzzy friend with big eyes rather than big fangs. I'm sure you'll agree that they aren't a bit like those other ruffian spiders, being inquisitive and bouncy rather than skulking and scampering. It has even been postulated by learned types that these charismatic creatures shouldn't really be called jumping spiders at all, and that perhaps a better moniker for these hydraulic furballs would be "eight-legged cats."

LEXICON

Arachnid

From the Greek for "spider"—which is itself attributed to the Greek myth of Arachne—"arachnid" is used to denote a group of animals that includes scorpions, ticks, and mites, and of course spiders.

AMAZONIAN GIANT CENTIPEDE

SCOLOPENDRA GIGANTEA

If a snake had the propensity to beef itself up a tad, we would wager it'd get some legs to move faster and slip into some battle armor to become impervious to blows. No doubt it would be the most terrifying snake in town, and would adopt the name "snakenator" or "snakeasaurus." The snake really wouldn't need to, though, because someone got there first, and thankfully they didn't give themselves silly names. Say "good day" to the Amazonian giant centipede.

Mammals love to eat arthropods. Bats can eat 100 mosquitoes in an hour, anteaters can slurp their way through 30,000 ants in a day, and aardwolves can have 200,000 termites licked in the same time. Even humans are pretty partial to them, with cultures around the world tucking into crunchy, leggy snacks, whether by choice—like the Chinese—or by proxy, like you or me. It is estimated that in Britain people get through a little over two pounds (1 kg) of arthropods a year, from the maximum allowable 340 bits of critters in a mug of hot chocolate, to the 12 allowable aphids in the hops in your pint of beer.

Not so the other way around, unless we've passed on and spent some time deep down in the ground, as we are just too bloody big for them. Sure, there are sneaky scamps that nip a morsel off us here and

"I'LL HAVE THE MAMMALIAN SOUFFLÉ FOLLOWED BY A SIDE ORDER OF TARANTULA ..."

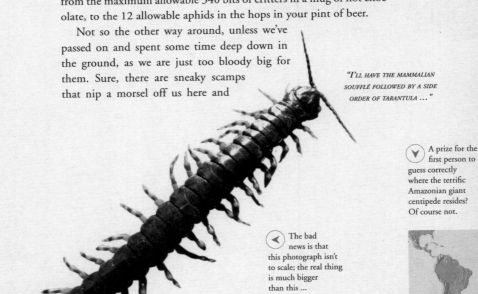

A prize for the first person to guess correctly where the terrific Amazonian giant centipede resides? Of course not.

The bad news is that this photograph isn't to scale; the real thing is much bigger than this ...

Millipede

The oldest known land creatures, millipedes (*Pneumodesmus newmani*) and centipedes scurried out of the big drink 428 million years ago. Soon after folks started saying "Do you know he hasn't got as many legs as he says he has?" and they were right ... the *milli* (thousand) *pedes* (feet) do not have a thousand feet, and a centipede can have anywhere between 20 and 300 feet.

"SORRY OLD BOY, MATH NEVER REALLY WAS MY BEST SUBJECT."

there like the mosquitoes or fleas. Still, to take down and eat one of our furry family of mammals a bug needs to be really big. Enter the Amazonian giant centipede, the biggest centipede in the world: it's as long as a man's forearm, as strong as a snake, and fast, armored, venomous, and rather unwelcome at most soirées. Just to clarify, it is not the biggest centipede that has ever lived; that would be the now extinct *Euphoberia*. There are also rumors of the Galápagos centipede reaching 2 feet (60 cm) long, but that has never been confirmed. Still, they would have to be rather ill-tempered to be as fearsome as the latter day Amazonian giant centipede.

Getting a Leg Up

What you really have to admire in this devil is his ambition. Not content with nibbling away on vegetation or other small animals like most of the arthropod world ... no no no ... he wants to eat the big tasty stuff. He is never happier than when he is chowing down a mouse, and will happily take down a tarantula for even daring to pretend to be big and tough. Even more impressively, it is the way he catches bats for supper that propels this smasher into our annals of the bizarre. One of his devilish ploys to get a bit of red meat is to climb to the top of a bat-infested cave and scramble up to the ceiling where he dangles his front end down into the bituminous abyss. Before long an unlucky bat will stray close enough to be grabbed and injected with enough venom to kill it in an instant. In only an hour the centipede will have gobbled the bat, down to the last mammalian morsel.

Fact

Euphoberia—*the largest centipede ever to have lived— was four times the size of his Amazonian counterpart, though thankfully he lived 250 million years ago. Bigger still was the near nine-foot (2.75-m)-long ancestor of both the centipedes and millipedes, the* Arthropleura, *which was the largest land invertebrate ever.*

FIRE ANTS

SOLENOPSIS SPP.

〜◆〜

How many fire ants does it take to change a light bulb? One to go up your leg and another couple of thousand to follow, swarm all over you, set about your tender parts with their fiery stingers, and not give a damn about your blasted light bulb. They are utterly inept at simple household maintenance, though don't for a moment think them daft.

Fire ants, also known as ginger ants, are a type of very small, yet very bloody annoying ant, with more than 280 species around the world. They are aggressive and, unlike many ants that bite and then spray acid over the wound, the fire ant only uses his jaw to latch on to some poor beggar, before injecting toxic venom into them with a stingy tail. The venom gives the sensation of being on fire, not surprisingly … well actually, rather bloody surprisingly if it happens to be you they are stinging. Small they may be, but the fire ants also have a rather impolite habit of synchronized biting; they crawl all over the victim, wait for the signal and, when one of them causes a bit of a stink in the form of a pheromone signal, they attack in unison, like a raging fire licking up your leg. You'd quickly realize what it would feel like if you were Joan of Arc and had thought it nice and comfortable to wear some particularly cheap polyester trousers for the big day.

"IT'S THIS BLOODY WAY YOU FOOL."

Nasty fiends these ants may be, but it is this swarming behavior that attracted us esteemed folk down at The Proceedings to them in the first place. Now, the human brain is a marvelous thing, and no one has got the foggiest how it works due to its bedazzling complexity: up to 100 billion neurons, with 1,000 trillion connections snapping and firing and blazing and coming up with all sorts of interesting whatnots, like itineraries and cummerbunds and light bulbs and hats

◀ Ants will do things randomly until they find a solution to their problem.

and merry little ditties. Coincidentally, 100 billion is exactly the number of galaxies in the entire known universe, so to sum up there are quite a few things going on in a human mind.

An ant's brain, of course, is much smaller than a human's—he can't even change light bulbs, never mind invent them. He scampers around with his tiny mind, doing as he pleases—no one is ordering him around. This doesn't stop ants collectively solving remarkably difficult conundrums, however: thousands of random actions hit upon an answer to a problem rather quickly. Indeed, we can adapt this swarm intelligence for ourselves and use it to simulate how crowds behave; in the future it is thought that it could be used to locate illness in the body and even to map planets. So while one little fire ant may be an insufferable buffoon, a whole group of ants can work out a problem quick smart. Who knows what sort of processes are going on in an entire nest of half a million ants: a multitude of ants with 250,000 neurons in their tiny minds; 125 billion neurons all snapping and firing and blazing to find all sorts of interesting whatnots. We should use our puny 100-billion-neuron-strong minds to find out a little bit more about what they are bloody well up to.

LEXICON

Neuron

Put simply, neurons are the main "thinking" cells of the nervous system. Each one looks like a numerously branched tree and may connect with hundreds of other neurons. Hundreds of billions of neurons all with multiple interconnections, combining to make 1,000 trillion connections. Not surprising then that the human brain is so complex.

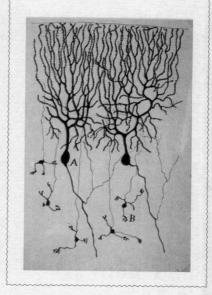

The fire ants were originally found in South America, but they've since decided to be a pain in other places.

"The ginger ant? What the blazes, I'm obviously auburn..."

CAMEL SPIDERS

ORDER: SOLIFUGAE

Gadzooks! In the world of creepy-crawlies, the camel spider is a right honorable lord of the realm. In fact we here at The Proceedings of the Ever so Strange would like to put forward that arachnophobes are only arachnophobes because they don't yet know about the camel spiders. Once they find out about camel spiders they quickly develop camelspiderophobia.

"Spiders? Pah! I had two for breakfast."

Camel spiders aren't actually spiders; they belong to the Solifugae and are more closely related to scorpions. Recent wars in the Arabian sands brought these buggers out into the public eye. The rumors didn't paint a pretty picture: a spider the size of a dinner plate that runs alongside speeding armored personnel carriers, screaming all the while. They chew on you while you sleep; they can jump three feet (1 m) high; and they can disembowel a camel.

The good news is that these are all myths. Unfortunately there is bad news. They run at about 10 mph (16 kph), which is incredibly fast for an oversized bundle of horror, and they really like shadows. So if they see one they will hurtle toward it—and yes, that does include yours—which isn't so much unnerving as pant-wettingly terrifying. They will readily bite you with the enormous pair of gnashers at the front, and a bite will leave you with a rather nasty ragged wound that is prone to infection. For an added *soupçon* of terror, those giant snippers also make a hissing sound when rubbed together.

The camel spiders can be avoided in the following localities.

One final thing about the camel spiders—they are known as "beard trimmers" by the natives as it is said that they like to trim your beard in your sleep. This is obviously nonsense, no matter how handy it would be, though it is quite often found that the camel spider's nest contains fur.

MIMIC OCTOPUS

THAUMOCTOPUS MIMICUS

Only recently discovered, this little octopus has caused quite a stir down at The Proceedings. Quite simply, she is an incredible impressionist, able to put the heebie jeebies up anything that might want to eat her. She can also pretend to be something nice and friendly, like a mate for a crab, only to gobble up the poor pinchy thing when it comes close.

Quite marvelous is the mimic octopus's ability not only to take on the shape, color, and texture of other animals but also to copy their movements. This is an extreme example of Batesian mimicry—you know, the thing you learned at school: flies that look like wasps, harmless snakes that look like evil snakes … that sort of thing. While most other animals adept at mimicry can only imitate one other species, the mimic octopus is able to imitate more than 15, including mantises, shrimps, stingrays, sea snakes, poisonous lionfish, crabs, flatfish, brittle stars, shells, and jellyfish. A supreme degree of flexibility is essential for such skullduggery, and our friends the octopuses are amazingly malleable.

These multi-talented, multi-legged mimics have another trick up their many sleeves. You see, these mollusks are very clever—they may be in the same phylum as the shellfish, but they definitely did not go to the same college. Octopoids are really rather bright, and our little friend the mimic octopus can pick her disguise according to the nature of the threat she faces, whether it's a snake or a fish. A really rather splendid little thing, I'm sure you'll agree.

> **Fact**
>
> *A mention should be given to another Indonesian resident, the coconut octopus, who unsurprisingly imitates a coconut and pokes out two of his tentacles to walk or float away. Although his repertoire is small, the coconut octopus really does appear to have perfected his disguise. The mimic octopus, however, while having a great repertoire, is said to do a truly dreadful impression of a pineapple.*

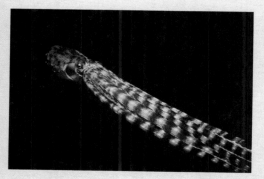

▼ Everybody loved seeing her impression of a sea snake.

▼ If your eyes are peeled, you might find the mimic octopus in the waters around Sulawesi.

TURBELLARIA

TURBELLARIA

Hell's bells! Meet the worst animal you could ever invite to the pub … the Turbellaria. The Turbellaria are a class of some 4,500 species of flatworm, which accounts for pretty much all of the free-living flatworms. Some species of Turbellaria do still lord around in other animals' bodies, acting like they own the place, but to be honest they represent rather ideal drinking companions compared to some of the other sods.

These flatworms tend to be rather small because they get oxygen by diffusing it into their bodies. The larger ones are rather flat for the same reason. Creatures tend to be the right shape or size, as a rather clever chap once said (Haldane's principle, p. 93). Although it is often said that earthworms can be sliced in half to make two individuals, that is a myth. Some species of Turbellaria on the other hand can be chopped in two without killing them, though why you would choose to have two of them accompany you to the pub is anyone's guess.

We haven't yet mentioned just quite why they are dreadful in public. Well, it is all about their

---

> ### LEXICON
>
> ## Platyhelminthes
>
> This is the real name for flatworms, though with them being flat and a worm, the Platyhelminth moniker has become rather unfashionable.

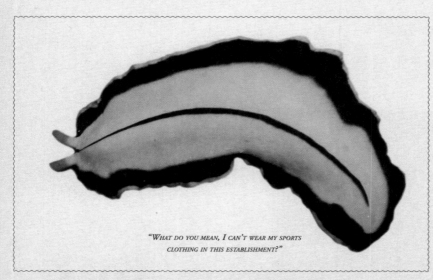

◀ Not only do Turbellaria act in a dreadful manner, they also have a questionable sense of style.

"What do you mean, I can't wear my sports clothing in this establishment?"

> Though they look like they are having a jolly nice time dancing, they are in fact "penis-fencing." One of them is about to chop into the other with its own very special type of sword.

> The Turbellaria are found in wet and moist places worldwide. Thankfully they refrain from attending most bars.

rather embarrassing mating behavior. They copulate by "penis fencing," the reality of which is worse than mere words can convey. Why they just can't ply each other with alcohol until they wake up in the other's bed with a faint feeling of bemusement and regret is beyond me. Turbellaria, you see, are hermaphrodites, meaning they are both male and female, and they penis fence to try to get the other pregnant. If one manages to stab the other with his mutton sword it will get them pregnant. The loser of the duel will have to carry around the other's babies, which is a bit of a disadvantage when each turbellerian is out to impregnate as many others as it can and so increase the number of its offspring. Who said romance is dead?

Better Out Than In

Naturally this sort of behavior is dreadfully embarrassing if you thought you were just going for a couple of ales and a game of billiards ... but it gets worse. The Turbellaria also lack an anus, which doesn't seem such a problem until you realize that they are simply going to vomit any "waste products." A rather unattractive trait in a potential suitor, I'm sure you'd agree. This could go half way to explaining why they need to threaten other turbellarians into having babies with them in the first place. So there we have it: the Turbellaria are marvelous chaps, just don't go out boozing with them.

Fact

The tapeworm, or cestode, is another type of flatworm and is among the biggest parasites on the planet. Somewhat discomfortingly, they can take residence in your gut and can grow to almost 70 feet (20 m) in some cases.

"DON'T LOOK AT ME LIKE THAT. I NEVER WANTED TO BE A TAPEWORM, YOU KNOW."

ASIAN GIANT HORNET

VESPA MANDARINIA

You know bees? Yes, the stingy little insects. Rather than the letter that comes after "A"s, the Asian giant hornet eats bees. They can eat as many as 40 in a minute and are quite simply bee sociopaths; a handful of Asian giant hornets can decimate a hive of 30,000 bees in the time it takes one to tuck into a rather hurried lunch.

The Asian giant hornets are huge evil buggers, the size of a small bird. What is more, they are fast (never a good thing in evil buggers), hitting top speeds of 25 mph (40 kph). Not surprisingly, native people tend to be a bit wary of them, calling them "yak killers" in the belief that they could take down animals as big as a cow. Folk from other areas call them the "sparrow bee," which is a mite more comforting until you realize that they are talking about how big the sod is rather than what it's capable of tussling with.

I can imagine that to you, dear reader, this is all beginning to sound fanciful and foolish. I suppose you think I am going to say something silly like its sting can dissolve human flesh. Well, cancel that trip to Asia, foolhardy adventurer, because that is exactly what its sting is capable of. The sting has been described as "like having a hot nail

> Unfortunately, this photograph is rather too close to the actual size of the Asian giant hornet for comfort.

"WHAT THE BLAZES ARE YOU LOOKING AT?"

> It may look like they are having an excellent time, but at the center of this ball is an Asian giant hornet.

"EVERYBODY PILE ON!"

The Asian giant hornet doesn't find it so much fun when the tables are turned. While he is happy to have a right old laugh killing a bee every other second, the native bees have a trick up their sleeve when it comes to attacking the giant hornets. They will swarm around the invaders—admittedly not the first tactic that comes to mind when face to face with a killing machine—and form a tight ball around it. The bees will then begin to vibrate their flight muscles until the center of the ball (the hornet) grows piping hot, oxygen levels plummet, and the evil creature inside is quite literally toast!

driven into your leg" by eminent maniacs who have decided to spend time researching them. It's not surprising that it hurts either—they are quite deadly, and the cause of more deaths per year in Asia than all the other animals put together, including tigers, bears, poisonous sushi, and snakes. The poison contains a number of compounds: some that dissolve tissue, others that cause pain, and at least one other that acts as an invitation to any other Asian giant hornets nearby to join in the stingy fun.

So what actually preys upon Asian giant hornets? Well, did we mention that the devil lives in Japan? Keen rivals to China in the "if it moves it must be food" stakes, the locals like to eat them deep-fried or as sushi, which sounds delightful. Not content with eating the slippery insides of the hornet, there is a very fashionable drink with an extract of giant hornet saliva. Olympic gold-winning marathon runner Naoko Takahashi swears by the stuff, saying it improves both endurance and the speed of her running. Well, if she thinks that drinking its spit makes her run fast, she should try being chased by one of them.

> The Asian giant hornet is found across a huge swathe of south Asia, though it is most common in the hills of Japan.

CHAPTER

2

FISH

Five hundred million years ago, a blobby creature was stuck to a rock feeling restricted by life. He imagined roaming the oceans freely, and began to change shape for this very purpose. Being wobbly wasn't ideal for wandering around the oceans, so he developed a stiff rod down his back. The backbone was to become *de rigueur*; indeed, the rest of our book is dedicated to this special blueprint.

First came the Agnatha, the jawless ones with rasping, sucking mouths that ate like your great-aunt Hilda. After years of not getting invited back to dinner parties, fish developed a jaw. All sorts of fishy forms soon evolved, including the sharks and rays, with their flexible skeletons, and the bony fish.

While some intrepid fish clambered up onto dry land, others admirably decided to stay put, happily living life in the wet stuff.

SABER-TOOTHED BLENNY

ASPIDONTUS TAENIATUS

Nothing nice ever had the prefix "saber-toothed." It is like putting "Democratic" in front of a country, or "Esquire" after a name. Still, what this swine lacks in being lovely, it more than makes up for in being ever so curious.

To tell the tale of the saber-toothed blenny, we first have to meet another denizen of tropical coral reefs: the bluestreak cleaner wrasse. He is a fine upstanding gentleman, everyone on the coral reef agrees, not least because he will happily slobber all over you, chewing away parasites and decaying flesh from your body. No prizes then for guessing that the bluestreak cleaner wrasse is a type of cleaner fish, with a blue streak down the side of it. They dot themselves around the reef at various cleaning stations and wait for a customer to dart along to this fishy equivalent of a barber's. These scrubbing stations can indeed be so popular that a polite queue forms. Yes indeed, fish have more manners than your average New Yorker.

To show he means no harm, the larger fish will adopt a docile, trance-like state, and the bluestreak cleaner wrasse will perform a dance to identify himself, before getting to work removing any excess mucus, dead scales, and parasites. Although it is really rather lovely, the little wrasse isn't doing this purely through goodwill; the detritus from the larger fish is like roast beef and mashed potatoes to

The bluestreak cleaner wrasse is the most popular fishy on the reef thanks to his work as an aquatic barber.

(LEXICON)

Selfish gene

The gene-centered theory of evolution is the current widely accepted theory of life on earth, at least among rational beings who believe the earth was made in more than a couple of afternoon sessions. It states that creatures are in fact merely vehicles for genes—genes that are trying to survive whatever the cost. It contributes to our understanding of a lot of things—for example why we help out family members, who share our genetic make-up.

"JUST A LITTLE OFF THE SIDE THIS WEEK PLEASE, STAN."

> The saber-toothed blenny pretends to be everyone's favorite fishy, the dastardly swine.

"WHAT DO YOU MEAN, I'M MORE BUCK TOOTHED THAN YOUR USUAL BARBER?"

Fact

Not only is the animal kingdom full of mimics (see mimic octopus, p. 57), it has found ways to cheat on virtually every level. To call an animal a cheat is of course dangerously anthropomorphic, but it's possible to detect a certain immorality: animals will scheme and connive whenever feasible in a bid to make sure their own genes are passed on. They will pretend to be something they are not to get a cheap meal, like the saber-toothed blenny or the anglerfish (pp. 66–7). They will masquerade with sham body parts to get out of fights, like the Australian crayfish that grow large but rather weak claws. Shrikes will cry wolf, raising a false alarm when there is food around in order to scare away other potential diners. Male cuttlefish will even look like a female in order to get one in the sack. Even in our own halls of academia, 70 percent of students admit to serious test cheating. Cheating is just doing what comes naturally to get ahead.

him. But how, I hear you ask, does this relate to our friend the saber-toothed blenny? Well, it turns out that he behaves in a rather similar manner to the bluestreak cleaner wrasse. In fact he mimics it. This saber-toothed scoundrel not only looks exactly like the cleaner wrasse, but behaves exactly like it, right up until the cleaning part, that is. Once the little dance to say "How do you do, sir, how's the wife?" is over, the fiend dives right in at the hapless fish, takes a jolly big bite out of the side of it, and buggers off before the fish can say "Ouch! I say, old boy, I think you've taken a nick out of me there." So there you have him: the saber-toothed blenny. I told you nothing good ever came from something starting with the words "saber-toothed."

"I SAID 'SHRIKE' NOT 'SHRIEK.'"

> The saber-toothed blenny can be found wherever the bluestreak cleaner wrasse is, namely on coral reefs throughout the tropical oceans. The bluestreak cleaner wrasse is said to be unhappy with the arrangement.

ANGLERFISH

FAMILY: CERATIIDAE

Fishing can be a lonely business; you sit around bobbing your lure up and down all day, no one to speak to or share a pipe with. The sea devil anglerfish pondered the problem and came up with a rather canny plan: to attach a mate permanently to her side.

Anglerfish comprise a number of species found throughout the world's oceans. Most live in the dank depths of the ocean. Some live on the bottom and look like they've been trodden on, while others are more free-swimming and look like they've been clapped between a pair of cymbals. Neither have of course, which is a shame as it might go some way to explaining why they look so bloody angry. While most of them do look greatly perturbed in some manner, all of them have a rather ingenious manner of perturbing other creatures. They are marvelously suited to chomping on things, not least because of their cavernous maw, packed to the rafters with rather pointy teeth.

> **LEXICON**
>
> ## Luciferin
>
> Luciferin is a type of light-emitting biological pigment used by the bacteria in the anglerfish's lure. In the Queen's English, and other inferior types of English, Lucifer generally refers to Satan. Though it is in fact Latin for "light bearer" and used to be more commonly used as a reference to the planet Venus, also known as the "morning star".

◀ The female anglerfish found the lack of light in the aphotic zone complemented her face rather marvelously.

▼ Anglerfish are found in the deepest parts of the oceans and seas, where it is dark enough for a luminous lure to make unprepossessing females look tasty.

Angling for Attention

Anglerfish are of course named after their chosen method of getting grub. You see, they spend their day waggling a very enticing wiggly thing around. Other fish think this is just splendid and soon skedaddle over to have a look. Of course most fish don't have time to think, "That tasty bit of grub doesn't appear to be a bit of grub at all; it seems to be a highly adapted dorsal fin filled with light-giving symbiotic bacteria and bobbed enticingly around so as to appear like a snack." In general they are far too busy being eaten to gawp at this particular evolutionary marvel.

The prey will also very rarely have time to remark how gruesomely ugly their attacker is. Indeed the predator is always a lady, at least the big bitey ones are. The male ... ah yes, we touched on this earlier ... the male is absolutely tiny. This chubby chaser's sole purpose in life is to amble around the ocean looking for a big lass to mate with. It is not an easy task being a male anglerfish, not least because the females are so awful-looking. It is rather difficult finding a mate down there in the inky depths—they are few and far between, and it is awfully dark. Thankfully the darkness negates the fact that they are awful-looking—we all know how quickly ugliness can be remedied by the flick of a light switch.

If the male is "lucky" enough to find a female anglerfish he jumps on her. No, not to ravish her, but to bite her and latch on to her side. He obviously quite likes it there as he simply withers away to a pair of testicles to fertilize her when she needs it, and no doubt to keep her company while she fishes merrily away.

The esca—the rod and lure that the anglerfish use—is in fact a highly adapted fin. It is the one that on most bony fish appears on the arch of the back. The anglerfish bobs and weaves the rod in all directions, and the bioluminescent lure can be seen for some distance in the bitumen-black abyss ... all the better to attract a potential victim. If a fish is daft enough to go up and chomp the end of the esca, the anglerfish's cavernous mouth is automatically triggered to snap him up.

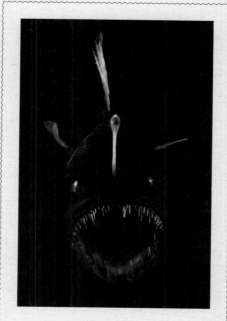

"Look who's come round for supper!"

BLACK SWALLOWER

CHIASMODON NIGER

The black swallower is a little fish with quite a claim to fame. How so? I'll give you a clue; it is not because of his dark coloration. This rapacious chap is an astonishing eater, able to nosh down another fish more than three times his own size. Much like you or I eating an entire deer in one gulp. He has of course learned a fundamental evolutionary lesson: where food is often scarce, eat as much as you can whenever you can get it.

We at The Proceedings can of course relate to this small fish's love of a big meal; it helps sober you up, prepares you for an evening drinking and is a wonderful accompaniment to lunch. Although the black swallower has never been seen alive, it has been hypothesized that the little rapscallion grabs his prey by the tail and then slowly "walks" his jaws up the still wriggling and quite probably rather vexed luncheon, much like a python eating an alligator. Of course, with no one having seen this take place, we haven't the faintest idea how he manages to turn the tables on such sizeable foes. Presumably the fish that is being chomped on puts up a grand old fight too, so how the black swallower isn't thrown off is a complete mystery.

In fact black swallowers are such gluttons they will take prey far too large for their stomachs to digest, their eyes being bigger than their bellies as it were. The hapless prey will end up rotting in the over optimistic cad's belly and the resultant gases will lift it up to the sea's surface like a balloon—killed by its own greediness. This doesn't even appear to be an isolated incident, as this is in fact how most samples of the black swallower are found. Quite worthy of the moniker, we are sure you'd agree.

Black swallowers can be found virtually worldwide, from the part of the seas where sunlight fails to penetrate down to the top of the deep bit known as the abyss.

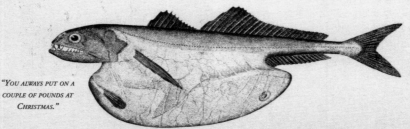

"YOU ALWAYS PUT ON A COUPLE OF POUNDS AT CHRISTMAS."

The huge extended stomach of the black swallower means it very rarely leaves food on the plate.

FRILLED SHARK

CHLAMYDOSELACHUS ANGUINEUS

———— ❦ ————

Hell's bells, has it really been that long? Meet the frilled shark—it's been a while since she's been invited to a soirée at the surface.

"IT REALLY IS DREADFULLY NICE OF YOU TO INVITE ME."

I can't believe it's been 80 million years already, it only feels like the last epoch … aaah yes of course, I remember now, it was back when the birds decided to get all pecky and gave up on the whole teeth idea. Still, it's good to have her back. The frilled shark was in fact thought to be extinct up until the 19th century, when a corpse washed up onto the shores of Japan. Of course, it is often said that many have been spotted since the Middle Ages; it is just that back then people quite reasonably surmised that they were sea serpents. Which is rather apt as, speaking of serpents, it is also hypothesized that the frilled shark strikes at its prey much like a snake snatching at a mouse.

One last curiosity I should mention about this remarkable and rather lovely shark: she gives birth to live young. It sounds odd, I know, but many species of shark do, and quite remarkably she has the longest pregnancy in the entire animal kingdom—twice as long as an elephant, in fact. For three and a half years she'll swim across the oceans and seas, carrying her young, until the big day arrives.

The sand tiger shark also gives birth to live young, but it is what happens inside mum's tum that is really rather intriguing—not to mention really rather sharky. The young develop in her womb, which is actually rather like a nursery, where they feast upon each other until one is full to the brim with brother and sister pie. Mom finally gives birth when the youngster is virtually full grown—about three feet (1 m) long—and ready to torment things other than his relatives.

Fact

The frilled shark would like to cordially invite you to stop by at any of her known residences dotted around the deepest seas.

COELACANTH

ORDER: COELACANTHIFORMES

In 1938 an acquaintance of ours, Miss Marjorie Courtney-Latimer, was alerted to a rather odd-looking fish that had been caught by a local fisherman. She declared it to be the most beautiful fish she had ever seen and so had it stuffed, badly. Miss Courtney-Latimer invited an eminent zoologist round to examine the catch. It looked bad, although not as bad as the last one of its type he'd seen—that one had been crushed into stone over millions of years.

The coelacanth has changed very little over the last 410 million years.

"I DIDN'T EVOLVE BACK IN THE LATE ORDOVICIAN AND I'M NOT ABOUT TO START NOW, SUNSHINE."

Coelacanths are found off the coasts of southeast Africa, Madagascar, the Comoros, and Sulawesi. They don't see why they should move; they've been there for hundreds of millions of years, don't you know.

The coelacanth is a living fossil: a modern fish that has close relatives in the fossil record from hundreds of millions of years ago. They have what look like the beginnings of legs—rather unusual appendages for a fish—and use them to walk around on the ocean floor looking for tasty morsels. What's more, it is because of these rather unfishy appendages that the scientific world is rather taken with them. You see, these lobe-finned fish, the family the coelacanths belong to, are thought to be very closely related to the ones that first scrabbled onto land to see what all the fuss was about. Of course, these intrepid explorers thought it was just smashing when they got there. They could evolve into man-eating lizards like the Komodo dragons, take to the skies like the storks, snuffle around underground like the moles, or just not look right, like the tapirs. They could decide that actually it was much better in the water anyway, like the sperm whales, start drinking the wet stuff like the vervet monkeys of St. Kitts, or discover that without the wet stuff, sex becomes a little different—just ask the bonobos.

Scaly Survivor

The coelacanth's brain occupies only 1.5% of the braincase; the rest is just fat. There are other odd things about him that point toward his primitive past, such as his tiny heart that is not much more than a muscular tube. He has evolved other capacities, such as the rostral organ—a unique structure that senses electricity and is probably used to detect prey. The coelacanth has hardly changed for nearly half a billion years, having lived through periods of history so tough that they make the extinction of the dinosaurs look like a walk in the park.

The coelacanth doddled along on his four fishy legs through the Devonian extinction event, which wiped out up to 80 percent of all species from the face of the Earth. He was around when the extinction known as the "Great Dying" happened, in which 90 percent of marine species were annihilated. When the Triassic–Jurassic extinction occurred, the coelacanth just sat by and wondered where everyone had gone, and why these new big lizardy neighbors were causing such a hullabaloo. When an asteroid popped a hole in the side of the planet, finishing off the dinosaurs and clearing the way for a certain bald ape and his chums, the coelacanth just carried on as he was, and there he's been for the past 65 million years. I suppose we've got some catching up to do.

These coelacanths are much like major extinction events; you wait 100 millennia for one to happen and two come along at once. Just a few years back a honeymooning marine biologist couldn't help but pop in to have a look around the local fish market. Propped up on a bit of ice was a new species of coelacanth. Undoubtedly, this resulted in a rather miffed new wife as they had to cart a large prehistoric fish around on their romantic getaway, although it no doubt raised a wry smile on the biologist's face.

▸ A coelacanth after a stint at the taxidermist's shop. He may look rather bedraggled but you should see his fossilized friends.

"I'D LIKE TO SEE HOW YOU'D LOOK AFTER 410 MILLION YEARS."

ANTARCTIC TOOTHFISH

DISSOSTICHUS MAWSONI

When water freezes it solidifies, crystallizes, and expands. The thing about hard, pointy, growing things is that they are very bad to have in your body. "Bursting" and "slicing" are two words that animals very rarely like to hear in reference to their body parts, and this is the very action that ice formations have on them.

"I LIKE TO COMPLEMENT YELLOW TEETH WITH A BROWN CRAVAT."

As a result, life usually heads to warm places without big icy pointy things to bother it. The life that does go to the Antarctic makes damn well sure it's equipped against being chopped up from the inside, none more so than the Antarctic toothfish. The Antarctic toothfish is a hefty specimen—about six and a half feet (2 m) long—that is found in the southern oceans. He is one of about 50 species of cod icefish. The cod icefish is quite unrelated to the tasty cod we enjoy in our fish supper, though he does taste quite like it, hence his other name, the "Antarctic cod."

The Antarctic toothfish is often thought of as a "cold-water" shark.

Gigantothermy

Gigantothermy is the theory that animals tend to get larger the farther you get from the equator. Of course, there are many exceptions to the rule, not least the fact that elephants like it where it is warm and are quite comfortable being big-boned. There does, though, seem to be some correlation, from the thousands of teeny tiny creatures swarming in the equatorial forests to the whopping whales of the poles. The so called "Bergmann's rule" was first noticed in 1847 by the German naturalist Karl Georg Lucas Christian Bergmann, who it should be noted was medium-sized.

In Cold Blood

The toothfish is often thought of as the cold-water shark, as he is one of the top predators of the Antarctic, chowing down any fish unlucky enough to get too close. He has got a cartilaginous skeleton like the shark, and is naturally a bit on the toothy side. Like the great white shark, the Antarctic toothfish has been subject to "gigantothermy." As a larger animal has less of its body close to the outside world, it is less troubled by the lack of heat around it. The seas of the Antarctic that he lives in are bloomin' freezing, although the Antarctic toothfish takes this brisk weather in its stride, even without a scarf. His metabolic rate is set at rock bottom—incredibly, his heart beats as slowly as once every six seconds. He sits in wait for most of his life, using as little energy as possible, and biding his time waiting for some dimwit to swim too close.

There is one thing in particular about this rather amazing fish, however, that propels it straight into our annals. Quite fabulously, he is able to produce antifreeze in his body that allows him to swim in water on the cusp of freezing. This incredible ability comes from a protein that moves freely around his cells. When an ice crystal starts to form, one of these proteins will come along and stick fast to it, thus preventing the crystal from growing any more. Which means that there isn't a hard pointy growing thing inconveniently making a mess out of this fish's body parts.

Fact

Antifreeze proteins are found in all manner of living things, including animals, fungi, bacteria, and plants. Though they have only recently been isolated, we are now beginning to see some commercial applications, including using it to make ice cream all nice and soft.

It won't surprise you to find out that these cold-blooded fish reside in the Antarctic.

This delightful stuff is soon to be introduced into your raspberry ripple.

FLYING FISH

FAMILY: EXOCOETIDAE

There are two things you should know about flying fish ... they are fish ... and ... oh, you've heard of them have you? Well, there are quite a few other things you should know about these rather ambitious creatures.

LEXICON

Exocoetidae

The family name of the flying fish, Exocoetidae, means "lying down outside." Back in the days of Pliny the Elder, it was thought that flying fish would come out of the sea and have a nice snooze on the beach at night.

Fish belong in water. A simple fact, you would think. But then again, why should they? Mammals have decided to plump on a pound or two and go for a bit of a splash around the ocean. What is more, they have decided to get all squeaky and creepy and take to the night skies. Birds have sometimes decided not to bother with all that "flapping about" nonsense and have taken to scampering around on the floor. So why shouldn't fish fly majestically through the air?

It is really a rather good idea too, this flying thing. The last place a fish-eater will have a look for a fish supper is in the air. Quite a good lesson in not getting eaten, I would say—do something very surprising and do it in a brisk manner. The flying fish, of which there are about 64 species, do their flying thing rather quickly too. It is one of the prerequisites of flight, unless you are talking about buoyant flight, and quite frankly an inflatable fish floating through the air like a hot air balloon would be just silly.

The flying fish needs to hit 50 mph (80 kph) to get lift, which is quite a task, though a peckish tuna breathing down his neck helps provide the necessary motivation. He gets up to speed by swishing his tail around 60 times per second, which is more like a vibration than a waggle. This phenomenal effort helps him to smash out of the wet stuff and into the dry air, where he cocks open his wing-like fins and soars off. Good show!

"NO ONE BELIEVED ME BUT I DID IT ANYWAY. NOW LOOK AT ME ... ALL IT TAKES IS A LITTLE DEDICATION."

The flying fish is found in all the world's big oceans. He is particularly partial to the warmer tropical and subtropical waters.

The flying fish's remarkable wingy fins help him achieve lift-off.

GOLIATH TIGERFISH

HYDROCYNUS GOLIATH

A huge bollard of darting fishy muscle, the goliath tigerfish is quite simply an eating machine.
Huge teeth are set into a hard bony jaw so that when he snaps his unbelievable trap shut they
interlock like a set of shears. If you are in the River Congo don't worry too much …
he'll only attack you if you're wet.

He's a beauty, isn't he! One learned friend of The Proceedings described him as "the fiercest fish that swims. Let others hold forth as advocates for the mako shark, the barracudas, or the blue fish of the Atlantic. To them I say 'Pish' and 'Tush'." Strong words indeed; however, we felt it prudent to establish just what a vicious brute he is. If you happen to have rolled up your trousers for a paddle in the Congo … it would be clever thinking to keep the noise down, as the goliath tigerfish's sense of hearing is absolutely tip-top. The other rather brilliant news about this highly astute, über-strong, man-sized, swimming set of interlocking gnashers is that they shoal … in huge numbers. Though we are rather pleased to be able to tell you that while attacks on humans have been reported they haven't as yet been verified.

"Jack the Kipper."

That said, there has to be a bit more than "bitiness" to get you into this exotic compendium of weird animals. You see, all around the world wildly different creatures can share common characteristics. One reason for this is that there are only so many things in the world that make a sufficient supper. What's more, evolution only has what it is given to work with—much like the Royal Family's portrait artist. The foot of an elephant contains the same bones as the foot of a mouse. The backbone of a giraffe has exactly the same number of vertebrae as that of Winston Churchill. The name for this, according to learned types, is "convergent evolution." "Why all these musings?" I hear you cry. Well, put simply, the goliath tigerfish is Africa's version of the Amazon river's renowned piranha—just bigger.

LEXICON

Red Queen's Hypothesis

The Red Queen's Hypothesis is the idea that animals are in a constant evolutionary arms race, the name coming from Lewis Carroll's *Through the Looking-Glass*, in which the Red Queen holds a race in which "It takes all the running you can do to keep in the same place." Prey evolves to be faster, and predators therefore need to evolve to be faster and bitier, which at least goes some of the way to explaining why the goliath tigerfish has evolved into a rather toothy torpedo.

These giant piranha can be found in the murky depths of the deepest river on the planet, the Congo.

COOKIE CUTTER SHARK

ISISTIUS BRASILIENSIS

Sharks are pretty pleased with themselves, and so they should be. You see, they are basically rippling slabs of muscle in gunmetal gray, with row upon row of huge razor-sharp teeth—awesome eating machines that have remained unchanged for millennia. And why should they need to change? They're perfectly adapted to what they do: when they're not eating seals like hors d'œuvres, they just like to cruise around the oceans looking like a whole barrel of tough.

Of course, some sharks don't look so tough. Think of the bizarre hammerhead, goblin, and frilled sharks. Not that they're to be trifled with. And then there's the cookie cutter shark, a sniveling little guttersnipe who looks more like a fat lady's arm holding a kitchen utensil than the pinnacle of predatory evolution.

Also known as the "cigar shark" and the "luminous shark," these are all rather soppy-sounding names for a little scoundrel who likes to get his meals in a rather devilish manner. Using his incredible powers of deception, he will think nothing of taking a chomp out of bigger fish. This is rather brave, but also rather sneaky and, like the anglerfish (pp. 66–7), it's all a question of using bioluminescence to lure prey—except in this case it's the absence of light-producing cells that the cookie cutter uses to get his meal ticket (see Lexicon).

Fact

Although the cookie cutter shark is dwarfed by the largest shark, the whale shark—a huge plankton-eater that grows more than 30 feet (10 m) long—the smallest shark is in fact the dwarf lantern shark, at less than 8 inches (20 cm) in length. He is said to have a terrible complex about it, too.

"OH RIGHT, YES, I'M A DWARF. VERY FUNNY. WELL, JUST FOR THE RECORD, I'M NOT HAPPY."

Pass Me the Toothpicks

It's worth noting that cookie cutters are one of the few sharks with a calcified skeleton. Most favor a cartilaginous skeleton, which is all nice and bendy for added flexibility and zipping around to chomp on things. Cookie cutters, however, have a calcified, bony skeleton (like ours). The reason for this is thought to be something to do with buoyancy. In itself, this may not sound worthy of a note in our almanac, until you find out that the cookie cutter actually eats its teeth. Sharks constantly replenish their teeth, and they grow and fall out like spiky passengers on an escalator to nowhere. Indeed, many learned types reckon that sharks can go through tens of thousands of teeth in a lifetime.

LEXICON

Bioluminescence

A lot of fish have cells along their belly that give off light. It's a rather clever way of not getting eaten, which most fish agree is a bit of a bind and they will try to avoid it if at all possible. If a big predator looks up from deeper water, these light-giving cells mean that our fishy friends aren't silhouetted against the sky, thus rendering them very nearly invisible—a shrewd move, I'm sure you'll agree. The cookie cutter sharks have taken this devilishly clever trick a step further. They have a patch of black near their throats that doesn't contain any bioluminescent cells. So predators see a tiny black speck above their heads darting around like a small fish. Not surprisingly, the predator bolts for the easy target—and this is when the pilfering swines pounce. Quick as lightning, they latch onto their attacker using their big rubbery lips. Their huge teeth—the biggest of any shark species relative to size—slice into the hapless bugger's flesh, nipping out a perfectly circular cookie-shaped bite.

Seeing as cookie cutters don't have much in the way of fishy skeletons, they don't get much in the way of calcium, and so have taken these rather drastic measures. Most other sharks simply let them drop to the ocean floor.

Speaking of skeletons, most sharks, metaphorically speaking, are almost entirely bone from the neck upwards. Cookie cutters are no exception to the rule and so often take lumps out of the wrong thing. Submarines, microphones, and electric cables have all been subject to the cookie cutter's fearsome chomp. Thankfully, only once has a human been on the receiving end of these fearsome gnashers. Big, tough sharks, on the other hand—the gunmetal-gray slabs of muscle that eat dolphins as an *amuse-bouche*—are often found with more than one big, cookie-shaped lump taken out of their considerable backsides.

"Doh ... Ray ... Mee ... Fah ... Soo ... Laa."

◄ Sweet little thing isn't he? The cookie cutter shark might look snuggleable, though we can confirm that it is a terrible idea to snuggle up to him and indeed a rather swift way of getting a circular chunk out of your buttocks.

► Now you know the places where these fearsome creatures reside, you may want to start spending your summers somewhere else . . .

OCEAN SUNFISH

MOLA MOLA

* ❦ *

The largest bony fish in the world is the incredible ocean sunfish, a bizarre circular fellow that can reach more than 13 feet (4 m) across, weighing up to 5,000 pounds (2,300 kg)— about the same weight as an Asian bull elephant—which is a lot, but please don't tell her I told you so as that would be terrible manners.

This enormous bony fish gets her name from the behavior of thermal recharging: basking her big flat body in the warmth of the sun's rays after periods spent in the depths of the chilly ocean. In fact, she has a number of rather apt monickers: in many countries she is known as the "moonfish"; in Germany she is "the swimming head"; in Poland she is the "head alone"; and in China she is the "toppled car," which makes absolutely no bloody sense whatsoever.

I am a simple man who likes to keep things elementary; I call the dog "doggy" and Lady Gwendolyn "darling." So I thought it pertinent to bring to your attention the fact that the word "fish" is somewhat misleading. There are nine different classes of vertebrates: mammals, birds, reptiles, and amphibians are a familiar and really rather nicely defined four of them. Incredibly, the other five are all different classes of fish. The Agnatha are a family of weird eel-like fish in a similar mold to the hagfish (pp. 80–1) and lamprey. The Acanthodii and Placodermi are types that didn't do frightfully well in the world and went extinct. The Chondrichthyes have cartilaginous skeletons, much like the lovely cookie cutter shark. Finally there are the more "fishy"

"How dare you, sir! I would riposte if I had the mental acuity."

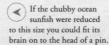 If the chubby ocean sunfish were reduced to this size you could fit its brain on to the head of a pin.

> I would wager that the first question asked once this huge specimen had been hauled onto dry land was, "Right, what now?"

"POSING NEXT TO VERY LARGE FISH WAS OBVIOUSLY A POPULAR PASTIME IN THE BYGONE ERA."

fish, the Osteichthyes, which includes tuna, cod, the leafy sea dragon (pp. 82–3), the black swallower (p. 68), the king of herrings (pp. 86–7), and our smashing ocean sunfish.

Thankfully the ocean sunfish doesn't care what you call her as she is a bit daft—possibly the silliest animal in the sea, after a giraffe of course. Her brain is quite literally the size of a peanut, weighing in at $1/6$ ounce (4 g). She doesn't really need a whopping great thinker of course; there's no pressing need for advanced calculus in the depths of the ocean. Nature is like that ... terribly efficient. The ocean sunfish happily wanders the oceans eating jellyfish and taking things easy. She eats the easiest of prey, including starfish, sponges, and anything else that can't get away from the slow-moving oaf, to be perfectly honest. So how did she get so big? Well, quite simply by eating lots and lots. All the really big animals around the planet have access to tons and tons of food. The elephant chows down on the grasses of Africa and Asia. The blue whale, who incidentally has a tongue the same length as an elephant's, slurps up tons and tons of krill. The ocean sunfish, the largest bony fish in the world, eats jellyfish and sponges by the bucket-load.

Fact

One of the smallest fish in the world, Paedocypris ("child carp"), hails from a Sumatran swamp and is the size of a grain of rice. Indeed he is the smallest vertebrate in the world. He lives in water almost as acidic as vinegar, lacks a skull, and has clasping claws that he may use to grab mates with. There is however one fish that is smaller—the male anglerfish (pp. 66–7)—but he is little more than a pair of testicles, while the female is rather large and quite a bruiser.

< The ocean sunfish can be found in any sea that is warm enough. He does feel the cold terribly.

HAGFISH

FAMILY: MYXINIDAE

*Deep in the oceanic abyss lives a rather gruesome creature.
The hagfish is, as you can imagine, a really rather beautiful creature ...
not really, he's bloody horrible.*

As I mentioned in the previous entry, there is a smattering of confusion as to what should be called a fish, and it is often said that the hagfish shouldn't really be lumped in with our scaly chums. For a start they don't even have a backbone like mammals, birds, fish, and reptiles; they have a skull but no spine. They have four hearts and two brains, which is more like a worm than a fish. What is more, their jaws do not articulate but instead move horizontally. They don't even have teeth, but instead have teeth-like structures made of keratin—the stuff that makes up our hair and nails, the rhino's horns, and the bird's feathers. The hagfish don't really have eyes either, just very basic eyespots, which is of great interest to my colleagues in the evolution department down here at The Proceedings.

These so-called slime eels aren't actually eels at all, though they are slimier than a used-car salesman. They can produce enough chemicals to turn a 5 1/4-gallon (20-ltr) bucket of water to slime in minutes, which is a really rather clever defense mechanism as all that slime would clog up a predator's gills, making them unable to breathe. It would probably also cause the preda-

Fact

Though it is very easy to say that they are a downright abomination, we can also say that hagfish are a very successful abomination. They have been unchanged for 300 million years, since about 65 million years before the dinosaurs decided to cause a bit of a hoohah.

"WHAT THE BLAZES? ARE YOU TRYING TO CALL ME CHINLESS AND SPINELESS? OH, ACTUALLY THAT'S FAIR ENOUGH ... "

Hagfish may look like an eyeless eel with whiskers, mainly because they are pretty much like an eyeless eel with whiskers ... just with no jaw or backbone.

Hagfish are found in a number of localities, though they are rarely highlighted as one of the "things to see" in travel literature.

(A) Hagfish don't just eat rotting whale carcasses. Their favored food is polychaete worms, the orange thingies in this photograph that are soon to be disappearing from the upper holes.

"BLAST IT! THEY ARE AROUND HERE SOMEWHERE—IF ONLY WE'D HAVE EVOLVED A DECENT BLOODY EYE."

The evolution of the eye, particularly the human eye, seems to create a problem for creationists who can't seem to get to grips with how something so complicated could suddenly appear by random chance. The simple answer is that it hasn't. Evolution works in increments; a tweak here, a knock there. The eye began with a single cell telling a creature whether it was light or dark, followed by a couple of cells to say whether it was a bit of a grim day. Soon enough something had evolved enough cells to tell whether a predator was hovering above and blocking out the light. This proved a very successful survival trick and, while its rivals were getting eaten, this fellow was spending a lot more time with the ladies. The ladies produced lots of babies and one of these babies' babies' babies mutated to have an ineffectual lens. The lens evolved to be rather marvelous, helping the chap to identify food and so grow big and strong. So it goes on: simple, elegant evolution.

tor to question whether dining on hagfish was such a bright idea after all.

These hideous denizens of the deep have a sluggish metabolism and can survive months without a feed, but when they do feed it is remarkably vigorous. They are one of the first fish to arrive at a whale fall (see bone-eating snot flower, p. 38), latching on to the dead whale, tying themselves into an overhand knot, and sliding the knot down their body to lever off a hunk of dead whale flesh. The majority of the hagfish's cuisine is not rotting whale meat, however, but worms. It is thought to be hermaphroditic—a fact that doesn't come as much of a surprise as I can't imagine one getting a date. Either way, bloody awful it may be, but it is also bloody marvelous. Huzzah for the hagfish!

LEAFY SEA DRAGON

PHYCODURUS EQUES

This is the leafy sea dragon ... there ... look ... he's right in front of your bleeding eyes!
Yes, that leafy dragon-shaped thing in the sea ...

This master of disguise can be found, if you look very hard, around the Western Australian coast. The leafy sea dragon is a teleost—a bony fish of the same ilk as tuna, minnows, goldfish, or cod. It doesn't look much like a plain old fish we are aware. This fellow is related to the pipefish (which looks like a pipe), the seahorse (a horsey-looking fish), and the weedy sea dragon (which looks similar to the leafy sea dragon, just less leafy). Like the pipefish and seahorses, the sea dragons have taken to paternal care of offspring, which means dad gets pregnant, as it were. This actually makes a lot of sense—mom can divert as much energy into producing as many healthy eggs as possible, and the eggs get a bit more care than if they were just dumped into the ocean currents. The female deposits about 250 eggs into the male brooding pouch, where they are nurtured for nine weeks. There they are fed, oxygenated, and most importantly protected from hungry predators. Once they hatch, it is every fish for itself, and only about five percent will survive the first couple of years.

Recently the Australian government decided it was high time to officially protect these lovely dragons. The leafy sea dragon has had a

"NOBODY HERE BUT US LEAFY THINGS."

The only part of the leafy sea dragon that moves are two fins on his back that are incredibly difficult to see. The rest of it wafts about in the current like seaweed.

Pipefish

The pipefish not surprisingly looks like a pipe, although not the sort for puffing on. They are instead long and thin for darting at prey like an arrow, though one or two have made a sartorial mark, as you can see.

The ornate ghost pipefish appears to be a rather spiky twig bobbing through the ocean currents.

We can only assume the harlequin pipefish has been at a more potent brand of absinthe.

"THAT'S WHY I'M RARELY FOUND IN A TOBACCONIST'S STORE."

bit of a rough time of late, not least from that bastion of buffoonery, Chinese traditional medicine.

Of course the particularly remarkable feature of this sea dragon is her absolutely incredible camouflage. True to her name, she has leafy protrusions that stick out all over her body, not for the purpose of moving around but rather to simply flutter in the ocean currents like a clump of seaweed. In fact the leafy sea dragon's bony body is quite hard, further hindering her motility. She moves by minutely undulating two tiny fins that are completely transparent so as not to upset the ruse. No prizes for guessing that this fish is not going to win any races, but thankfully no one would be able to see her and realize she had actually entered into the competition.

You can be blissfully unaware of the presence of a leafy sea dragon around Australia from Kangaroo Island as far up as Julien Bay.

Fact

The pygmy seahorses are the smallest of the Syngnathidae, the family to which the pipefish, the sea dragons, and the seahorses belong. They really are tiny, too—about the size of two peas stacked on top of one another—though no one knows how many species there are, which is probably due to them being so small and so blasted hard to find.

"FRIENDS CALL ME THE SEA PEANUT."

CLOWNFISH

FAMILY: POMACENTRIDAE

Clownfish have had it good of late … world-famed actors and media darlings, they are the fishy toast of Tinseltown. What those Hollywood types didn't tell you, however, is that these chaps want to be chicks. Of course, we at The Proceedings of the Ever so Strange are liberal-minded souls and we salute transvestism. For one thing, we think it takes balls.

The clownfish, also called the anemone fish, lives in symbiosis with a clown … damn … sorry… anemone. Anemones are big stingy devils, making an anemone a rather unusual place to put your fins up after a hard day. What's more, the anemone's stinginess deters would-be predators from popping in for a snack, making them quite simply safe as houses. The anemone gets a good deal too; what with all that swimming back and forth keeping the water circulating, the clownfish helps clean its host. As if that wasn't enough, he also gets to eat all the fish poop. Positively delicious!

"Eat, drink, and be Mary."

Naturally, living in stingy things isn't the really remarkable thing about the clownfish. You see, what every schoolboy clownfish wants to be when he grows up isn't an astronaut or a train driver. What "he" wants to be is a "she." All clownfish are born as males and remain tiny pre-pubescent fellows until it's time for their big transformation. Clownfish live together in a group made up of a dominant male, a female, and their young. When the female dies the dominant male takes the unprecedented step of turning into a dame. He, soon to be a she, will take on all the duties of the female, including laying eggs. Soon the male fish will start to look differently at their old mate Percy, and one of them will grow into an adult male and form something really rather cozy with her.

Do pop by and say hello to the clownfish if you are in the neighborhood, though don't get too carried away; remember, she used to be a chap.

BLOBFISH

PSYCHROLUTES MARCIDUS

This curmudgeonly fish lives deep in the abyss around the coast of Australia. What's more, he's made almost entirely of jelly—yes, really, though that doesn't seem to have cheered him up, and it should be noted that he really doesn't go down that well with ice cream at children's parties.

One of the problems with living in water is that it is very hard to stay where you are. If you are a little bit heavier than water you will sink, and if you are bit lighter you will float up toward the surface. Of course, having to fight against this all the time would be a bit of a chore, so fish have evolved bladders full of air to help them retain a neutral buoyancy. The problem is that gas-filled organs aren't really the best idea under the immense pressures of the abyss and so the blobfish has evolved a different method of maintaining neutral-buoyancy. The portly fellow's jellied flesh is in fact around about the same density as water, which means that he doesn't have to use up any energy if he doesn't need to. This is handy because the blobfish doesn't get to eat much, relying on infrequent scraps from the life-rich upper ocean that happen to drift past his nose.

An ugly and lazy blob of jelly he may be, but he has evolved rather neatly to fit his ecological niche. Although he isn't going to woo himself into the upper echelons of Park Avenue society, he is in his element blobbing around at the bottom of the ocean.

The related fathead is said to be equally annoyed about his moniker.

The blobfish is found in the deep waters off Broken Bay in Australia. Don't drag him up to the surface, he really doesn't like it.

"... WE WILL FIGHT THEM ON THE BEACHES."

Damnations, it appears as if my Winston Churchill bust has melted. Oh no, it's just a blobfish.

KING OF HERRINGS

REGALECUS GLESNE

—◦◦◦◦◦◦—

We only really know a smidgeon about this most marvelous-looking beastie,
the king of herrings. He is a huge serpentine fish of sparkling silver, resplendent
with a crown—an oceanic majesty.

What we can tell you is that the king of herrings is the world's longest fish, reaching lengths of up to an incredible 39 feet (12 m). He is a type of oarfish and more than one researcher has said that he gives off electric shocks when touched. A group of deep sea divers recently reported that he moves by undulating the enormous fin along his back, keeping his body quite straight. Other than that, it is fair to say we know almost nothing about this beauty. So when it came to an evening talk on this king of herrings we were rather stumped as to what to say. Many people, new-age types mainly, wag their finger at us men of science and point out that we think we've got it all worked out. Well no, we haven't, it is actually quite the opposite. We are rather fascinated by this wonderful and intriguing place we call home and are fully aware how little we know about it. This of course led us to chat about what we don't know about, a subject that could fill this book many times over.

▼ In 1808 in Scotland a 56-foot (17-m) sea serpent was washed onto a beach. It is thought to have been a rather large king of herrings.

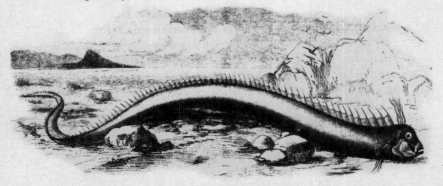

"Stop sketching me and get me back in the sea you oaf. Don't you know who I am?"

Homo ignoramus

We hardly know anything about the Universe; most of it appears to be missing, for starters, and the whole thing should be falling apart, but it isn't. We haven't got a clue if there is life out there, though according to the Drake equation there should be about 10,000 life forms in the universe who have the ability to communicate, and therefore countless others. We don't even know about our planet: what the weather will do from day to day, or when a volcano will erupt or the ground will shake. We haven't got the foggiest how many organisms there are; at best guess we think there are somewhere in the order of between five million and two hundred million. We don't know about what is at the bottom of the ocean or what made a huge noise there in the summer of 1997—a noise that was heard by sensors 4,800 miles (7,725 km) apart and was almost certainly organic in origin—a noise that could only have been made by something much bigger than any living thing ever known.

While it is not known whether herrings recognize their rather elusive head of state the king of herrings, the unrelated herring are smashing chaps in their own right. They fart to each other as a rather ingenious method of communication, although you have to wonder how they excuse themselves.

"ONCE FOR YES."

We don't know what causes ice ages every 100,000 years although we do know the planet's temperature only drops by two degrees Celsius; indeed we are actually in an ice age now. We certainly don't know what will happen as temperatures rise by a predicted four degrees in the 21st century. We don't know why humans kiss. It is certainly not genetic; there are theories that it dates from ancient times when a mother would mush up food for the little ones in her mouth, but who could ever know. We don't even know why we love. Although we at the Proceedings of the Ever so Strange would love to know about love, whopping great fish, weather, and aliens, we're also looking forward to finding out just a smidgeon about them.

Not surprisingly we haven't got the faintest idea what the distribution of this regal kipper is.

This marvelous specimen, discovered floating on the surface of the Pacific Ocean by a U.S. Navy boat in 1996, shows how bloody long the giant king of herrings can grow.

"I SAY, PUT ME DOWN OR I'LL GET MY MINIONS ONTO YOU."

CANDIRU

FAMILY: TRICHOMYCTERIDAE

What's worse than finding a worm in your apple? That's right, finding a fish in your John Thomas! Or even having an apple in your worm?! It was only a matter of time until we got around to this little terror—just pray that this terror never gets around to you. Meet the candiru, the most feared fish in the Amazon River.

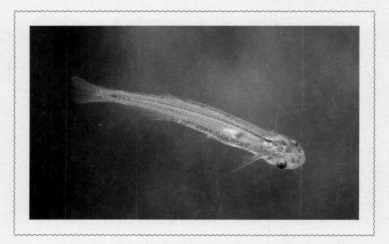

"PIRANHAS ... PAH!"

The candiru has a very anti-social habit: he follows streams of urine up into the urethra—the tube in your private parts—which delivers a lot of hurt. An eel-shaped catfish, about 6 inches (15 cm) long and about ⅖ inch (1 cm) thick, the translucent little rapscallion lies in wait at the bottom of the river. If he smells urea—the leftovers from when your body has metabolized protein—in the water, he will dart towards the source. Thankfully, humans aren't his usual prey. In fact the scoundrel is trying to get into the gills of some hapless fish. There he will spring his spines and gnaw a hole toward a major blood vessel, gorging himself on blood for no more than a few minutes. After a delightful liquid lunch, he will sink to the riverbed, and cogitate merrily until his next victim wanders past.

A Fish Out of Water

If he's very unlucky, the victim may be someone who is urinating into the river. It is really not the little fishy's fault—and the candiru would like it stated on the record that he'd rather not be stuck up to his tail in your privates—but he mistakes the urea in urine for a fish's gill excretions. You will be very pleased to hear that he really does go right in, so that all you can see poking out is his flapping tail, which is undoubtedly one of the worst sights in the animal kingdom. What is more, the fishy fiend sticks out a spike so it can't come out, even if you ask it really, really nicely, and offer it all sorts of cash incentives. Surgery is probably the only option, though local tribes say there is a pair of local herbs that can be inserted into the urethra to kill the fish so it will fall out. Just in case you are ever unlucky enough to come face to genitals with this cad, they are the jagua plant and the buitach apple, presumably not the whole apple though … apple … in your worm … oh never mind.

Catfish are a rather diverse bunch of fishes found in seas and freshwater all over the world. There are catfish that are stingy enough to kill you, and electric catfish that have rather shocking behavior. The cuckoo catfish lay their eggs in others' nests so that they can grow up protected in their oblivious foster mum's mouth. Walking catfish can walk and glass catfish are translucent. Catfish are rather remarkable for their range in sizes too, from the South American catfish that reach adulthood at ⅖ inch (1 cm) long, to the Mekong giant catfish that can be 10 feet (3 m) long, though thankfully they rarely try and swim up your willy.

"My cousin?
A dreadful boor …"

a. *Geniulata, Jagua Arnut.*
b. *Genipa, seu Janipaba.*

Dear reader, for your own sake take a good look at these plants and commit them to memory. They may come to your rescue the next time you are bathing in the Amazon River.

You can find the candiru in the River Amazon. At least, that's where he's hopefully decided to stay.

CHAPTER

3

AMPHIBIANS

Deep in the drink, millions of years ago in the middle of the age of fishes, something altogether less fishy was developing. Yes, they were scaly, and undoubtedly went rather well with a parsley sauce, but they were altogether more "walky" than the fish. After hauling themselves out of the water, they developed all sorts of fabulous stuff like lungs and legs and only had to return to the wet stuff to have young.

The amphibians spread out and changed shape to suit, evolving into the frogs and toads, the salamanders, and the rather odd limbless caecilians. It's fair to say, if it weren't for these intrepid pioneers, we wouldn't be where we are today—all high and dry.

In fact, may we propose that the next time you do bump into one of our amphibian friends you buy them a drink.

CHINESE GIANT SALAMANDER

ANDRIAS DAVIDIANUS

———— ◦◦◦◦◦ ————

Traveling around the globe, you'd rightfully expect to meet people of all shapes and sizes; what you wouldn't expect to meet are bloody great amphibians the size of humans. The giant salamanders of Japan and China are just two of some 500 species of salamander. The rest are found all over the world, from the tropical rainforests to the Siberian steppe.

O f course, it is not the icy steppe that salamanders are usually associated with, but fire. Leonardo da Vinci, among other bearded types, thought the salamander was born from fire. Naturally, there is a reasonable explanation for this, which is that these gentlemen like to hang out in wet logs, piles of firewood included, and the poor things are simply escaping from the flames after they've been thrown into the fireplace.

It is skedaddling that really sets the amphibians apart from the fish, of course, as it was these blokes' ancestors that were the first vertebrates to have a bit of a breather. Moving out of the water needed some big changes, the most obvious being four legs to walk on. They also needed to breathe in dry air, and so developed lungs; little more than a pair of teeny balloons they may have been, but they were good enough to keep these animals moving.

Representatives of these ancient colonizers include a giant salamander first brought to the attention of western science by a certain Johann Jakob Scheuchzer. The Swiss physician was rather taken by a fossil of one and, after careful consideration, named it *Homo diluvii testis* (Latin for "evidence of a diluvian human"), as he believed it to be of a man who had died in the Biblical flood … the buffoon.

Fact

It was actually a fish that first popped out of the primordial wet stuff to see what all the dry-land fuss was about. Such creatures were called fishapods, *which were fish in all respects apart from having front appendages rather like a crocodile's, with shoulders, elbows, and wrists.*

"*I MAY LOOK SMALL ON THE PAGE, BUT YOU'D RATHER I DIDN'T CHARGE AT YOU FROM A PILE OF FIREWOOD.*"

There are a smattering of these fellows left in some mountain streams in China.

CAECILIANS

ORDER: GYMNOPHIONA

Although the caecilians look like the product of a racy night betwixt a liquorice whip and an earthworm, they are in fact rather closely related to the frogs and salamanders. You'd be forgiven if you haven't seen one of these customers hanging around because they are rather elusive, spending the best part of their lives underground. Not surprisingly, they are rather shortsighted and can only just make out the difference between light and dark, even with reading glasses.

The caecilians grow up to five feet (1.5 m) long, and all but one species have a pair of lungs. One lung is bigger than the other so it fits better in that lithe body. This may seem unusual to those of us who like to sport two nicely balanced lungs, but snakes have similarly odd-shaped organs. It might interest you to know that the single caecilian species to not have lungs is rather a small chap. He doesn't need lungs because he can get oxygen deep enough into his tiny system through his amphibious skin—a rather fine example of Haldane's principle.

If you are rather determined to say good day to a caecilian you may pop over to a number of wet tropical regions around the globe.

It is rather easy to mistake a caecilian's head for his *derrière*, as he is disguised to look that way. If a predator thinks of taking one of these fellows out sharpish by munching on his head, he may bite on the head-shaped tail instead, leaving our amphibian friend to wriggle off into the sunset once again.

Less happily, some caecilians like nothing more than to eat their mother. Yes, these little wrigglers begin in the womb, chomping away at the lining. Some species even continue to eat their mother after they are born, tearing chunks from her skin and greedily gobbling them down.

"MMMM ... TASTES JUST LIKE HOW MOM USED TO MAKE IT."

Young caecilians chomping on their mother. Don't worry, she's quite unharmed.

(LEXICON)

Haldane's principle

Put simply, body size defines what body parts an animal needs. For example, large creatures need to develop complicated systems to get oxygen into their nether regions, whereas tiny creatures just absorb it through their skin. So as Haldane's principle predicts, a big caecilian has had to evolve lungs and a little one has in fact done away with them.

OLM

PROTEUS ANGUINUS

———❦———

This odd fellow lives in the Balkans, where he dwells in the cave systems that criss-cross the region. Back in the days when a squashed frog was the highest denomination of currency, if a particularly heavy rain broke the olms would spew forth from the caves. The locals thought that they were the young of enormous serpents living deep underground, but then the locals were equally aghast at those newfangled horseless carriage thingies.

The olm does look rather like a baby dragon that needs to get out and see some sunshine.

"It's not my fault, it's like a British summer down here old boy—no sunshine."

The olm can be found spooking the locals in the Dinaric karst of Southern Europe. What do you mean, you don't know where the Dinaric karst is?

The olm scuttles about in less-than-salubrious "venues," where his body has adapted remarkably to the lightless surroundings. He has a pinkish appearance, as he has very little need for color in the black belly of the earth. These pasty scoundrels also lack eyes—again, why waste energy on growing eyes when there is no light to see by?

So the olm has become a master at energy conservation when it comes to growing parts, but he also tries to take it easy in order to survive in the dark emptiness of the caves. The olm doesn't even have the energy for a bit of nookie. No need for all that strenuous to-ing and fro-ing, egg producing, and whatnot; no, that would be silly. In fact, an olm waits about 14 years before he even thinks of doing anything carnal, and he may even live for over 100 years to be sure of raising young.

Electroreception

Many creatures have evolved "electroreception" as a way of communicating, finding their way around, or locating food. Not surprisingly, it is more common in aquatic environments than on dry land, the wet stuff being a much better electrical conductor than air. It is for this reason that sharks attack underwater cables—the silly beggars.

A Sensitive Soul

Don't think for a moment, though, that these little oddities are helpless. Quite the contrary. For starters, they are covered in an incredible array of senses that pick up anything that might wander into the cave. Most things try to avoid falling into very dark caves, making food something of a rarity in such places. To ensure it doesn't miss an elusive meal, the olm is covered in sensors that pick up vibrations from anything that moves in the water. Even more incredibly, the olm is also covered in taste buds, like a great big autonomous tongue flopping and lolling around the cave trying to taste out prey. As if being able to taste and feel your prey isn't enough, the olm has developed electrical receptors, detecting the minute electrical pulses that living animals emit.

So if anything is silly enough to plop into the dank darkness of an olm's cave, you can be assured that this chap will find it. Even if he doesn't, it has been noted by learned types that he can last as long as six years without a meal. Added to the autonomous tongue business, this makes the rather unusual olm a grand addition to our marvelous menagerie of curious creatures.

Fact

In the West there are traditionally four taste sensations (sweet, salty, sour, and bitter), while in the East there are a number of additional components, such as spiciness from chilies and umami, or savory, from meats, cheese, and the like. The evolutionary advantages of taste are obvious: we are drawn to things our bodies need, like fats, salts, and whatnot, and driven from things that may be poisons, like bitter plant alkaloids.

◀ The Postojna cave system in Slovenia is the longest of its kind in the world. Plenty of room, then, for the olm to practice the art of living in such splendid darkness.

LAKE TITICACA FROG

TELMATOBIUS CULEUS

High in the South American Andes sits an epic body of water. Many years ago, the local tribes saw that it was shaped like a puma pouncing on a rabbit and named it Lake Titicaca. Later, Victorian naturalists found a rather curious-looking frog deep in its azure waters. They marveled at this new species, poked at its flaps of skin, scratched their learned chins, and decided that there was only one name for this froggy fellow: Telmatobius culeus, the aquatic scrotum.

The Lake Titicaca frog in its natural environment: Lake Titicaca.

Lake Titicaca is an unforgiving place. At nearly 13,000 feet (4,000 m) above sea level, the sun is punishing, oxygen is thin, and freezing temperatures abound. It is for this reason that the Lake Titicaca frog has evolved into something that looks like it should be in a man's pants, which is surprising, as a man's pants are rarely thought of as an extreme environment. It seems the key to the frog's survival in this harsh habitat is that it stays underwater at all times, and those folds and flaps of skin help with the uptake of oxygen from the lake.

Lake Titicaca sits on the border between Peru and Bolivia, in South America.

For years, this fellow has been revered by the locals, who think that he can summon rain. They take a frog, place him in a jar, and leave him at the top of a hill. Of course, the frog screams bloody murder. He didn't evolve into a scrotum-like frog just to sit in jars at the tops of hills—he much prefers life at the bottom of a lake where people can't constantly remark on how funny he looks. Unfortunately, the Froggish for "Get me out of this jar, you fools" must sound a lot like the Quechuan for "Oh, do rain, it would be awfully nice." Thankfully, sometimes the rains do come, and as the jar fills with water the frog can escape and go back to the bottom of the lake, where he feels much less self-conscious.

Frog Shake

When early explorers outfitted with the right apparatus visited the lake they reported that the bottom was quite literally swimming with "thousands of millions" of giant frogs, many up to 20 inches (50 cm) long. Sadly, the days of these behemoths have gone; there are few frogs left, and those that are still alive rarely get that big. One of the main reasons for their demise is the fad for "frog juice" in the nearby Peruvian capital, Lima. These cosmopolitan, forward-thinking, erudite types think that they can produce an aphrodisiac by skinning a frog alive, mixing it with a bit of honey and some roots, and whizzing it up in a blender. Of course, everyone knows nothing gets your beloved in the mood quite like watching a frog being skinned alive and then blended.

Fact

The Uros are a pre-Incan people who live at the center of Lake Titicaca. "Ah," you might be thinking, "You mean an island at the center of Lake Titicaca." Remarkably not, because they live on floating manmade islets, which they build by layering reed on top of reed, making a floating (and slowly rotting) platform. The Uros graze cattle, build houses, and even have fires atop stones on the reed islands. It's not a bad plan, either, especially if you have marauding, bloodthirsty conquistadors beating a path toward you—all you need to do is pull up the anchor and move not only your house, but the entire village.

> Take a good look at this delightful scene. By tomorrow the island will have floated out of view.

CHAPTER

4

REPTILES

Long before the birds got in a bit of a flap and the mammals were all hot under the collar, and millions of years before the dinosaurs stomped around our insignificant blue dot, there were a couple of four-legged fiends who couldn't bear to be around each other anymore.

One of these ancient stompers gave rise to the mammals. The other had a family bigger and more full of oddities than the cutlery in an old lady's drawer. He also had another family branch—the reptiles—which was a mishmash of cold-blooded fellows. Among them were the crocodiles and the *Sphenodon*, the turtles and tortoises, and the snakes and lizards.

All this because two ancient stompers just couldn't get on any more.

JESUS CHRIST LIZARD

BASILISCUS VITTATUS

The Jesus Christ lizards are so named because whenever anyone sees them run across water they point and yell, "Jesus Christ! What the blazes does he think he's doing?!" These extraordinary creatures are actually a rather smashing group of little reptiles found from Central Mexico to Ecuador—the basilisks. The word derives from the Greek basiliskos, "little king," which refers to the fold of skin on top of its head that looks like a crown.

Jesus, of course, was also famous for turning water into wine, which doubtless didn't harm his chances of enlisting new followers back in the day! The Jesus Christ lizard would be a lot more popular in civilized society if he could turn his hand to this particular miracle—not with this particular naturalist, you understand, as I have already turned my family fortunes, country estate, and townhouse in Kensington over in pursuit of booze.

"I CAN ALSO HEAL LEPERS AND POINT OUT BURNING SHRUBBERY, BUT I THOUGHT IT IRRELEVANT."

Of course, the most incredible thing about these fellows is that they can walk on water. The rainforests of the Americas are packed to the rafters with creatures that don't care much for religious lizards of any denomination and will quite happily have them as brunch rather than be amused at their apparent miracle-working, so the basilisk has learned to run faster than a lawyer after an ambulance. They run solely on their back legs, the bipedal motion helping achieve the necessary speed for such a miraculous feat. Their huge feet splay out to reveal frog-like webbing that stops them from breaking the surface tension of the water, and also creates an air pocket. Incredibly, they can stay on the surface for as far as 60 feet (20 m). Remarkable stuff!

(LEXICON)

Bipedalism

Moving around on two feet has a number of distinct advantages. In the case of the basilisk, it allows them to go that little bit faster, meaning that they can hoof it across the wet stuff. Bipedalism also raises your head so that you can have a good goggle at what is going on, and frees up the front limbs for flying, punching things on the nose, pipe smoking, and whatnot.

The brown basilisk can be found performing petty miracles in a number of Central and South American countries.

FLYING SNAKE

CHRYSOPELEA SPP.

❦

A number of animals have developed the ability to throw themselves off high things, hurtle toward the ground, and then miss. All of them have adapted some sort of device that helps them glide. There are flying squirrels who have big flaps under their arms, lizards who have big ribs that stick out, frogs with huge parachute-like feet. But in the world of these arboreal animal gliders, the flying snake is king.

Although they are called "flying snakes," they can't, in fact, fly. They glide. If you chopped one of these fellows in half you would notice that he looks just like a Frisbee's cross section. (Actually he'd look more like a really annoyed flying snake if you chopped him in half, but his cross section would nevertheless be Frisbee-like.) Rather good at gliding they are, too, with a four-to-one glide-to-drop ratio—that is to say, they travel as far as four feet (1.2 m) for every foot (30 cm) that they fall.

> *Most of these rather amazing gliding-rather-than-flying animals have evolved in the Asian rainforest. This is no coincidence, since the trees there are farther spaced out and so require a bit of lateral thinking—and, indeed, moving.*

Where they land is very much a question of ballistics. They simply make their decision before leaping out into thin air. Why they do it is another question, though the answer is rather simple: it's a good way of getting around as it takes up very little energy to move large distances and it is also a rather good way of getting away from anything that might want to eat a flying snake.

Fact

◄ The flying snake in the middle of throwing himself out of a tree.

"IT'S ALL SUCH FRIGHTFULLY GOOD FUN."

► Flying snakes are found in southeast Asia up trees, and sometimes in the air.

GHARIAL

GAVIALIS GANGETICUS

———❦———

The gharial is the strangest of the crocodilians—and that's saying something, because they're a strange bunch. Don't believe me? Invite them to your place for a drink. I assure you that it will be an unforgettable evening.

Fact

Although the whole Chixculub, death-by-asteroid theory is now widely accepted, it may be that the dinosaurs were decimated not by something from outer space but by a rather epic bit of global warming caused by the Deccan traps in India, one of the largest volcanic features on earth. Though the evidence is rather compelling for a meteor strike, the reasons the dinosaurs went extinct may well be multifaceted.

The gharials. Quite charming fellows. Somehow these cads, along with the rest of the crocodiles, lived through the cataclysm that wiped the better part of the dinosaurs off the face of the earth. This is super news, because at least we still have one ancient monster in town. Of course, we still don't know for certain how the dinosaurs were wiped off the face of the earth in the first place. The most likely theory is that a huge lump of rock banged into the planet, and indeed there is the evidence of a big wallop around Chixculub in Mexico, not to mention a load of asteroid matter found all around the planet in a layer at a certain point in time. So for the sake of argument, we will stick with this asteroid story for now.

➤ The pot or *ghara* at the end of the male gharial's nose develops with maturity. He uses it to blow bubbles to impress the ladies.

"YOUR PLACE FOR A G AND T? RATHER!"

Death to Fussy Eaters

This theory is rather helpful when it comes to explaining why it is that we are lucky enough to have the rather smashing gharial with us today. We do know that after the asteroid hit our planet virtually all plant life was put on hold as the Sun was blotted from the sky. This didn't bode well for the herbivores, who, not surprisingly, promptly starved to death. Moving up the food chain, the predators were also destined for the chopping block once their vegetarian chums were wiped out. However, animals that ate rotten and dead stuff had a simply marvelous time of it. Similarly, animals that lived in streams and rivers weren't as badly affected, as they were more dependent on food being washed downstream than anything else. Both of these factors suited the crocodiles rather well, as they live in streams and would eat the scabs off a fly-bitten donkey if they were even a trifle peckish.

The gharial on the other hand has had plenty of time to evolve into something much more sophisticated. He doesn't have an impeccable knowledge of the wines of the Bordeaux region and is said to be awful at the waltz, but he is a remarkably sophisticated fish eater.

Up to 20 feet (6 m) long, this most aquatic of the crocodilians is not small. What is more, he is really rather well suited to the wet stuff. Not surprising then he eats fish that are too fast for most crocs. That is also why he has this huge, long, thin snout rammed full of razor-sharp teeth. He lies in wait with these toothy swords ajar, and when a fishy dish pops by … snap! If his snappy trap isn't working, he'll use his flat, paddle-like tail to slip through streams and whack unsuspecting fish onto the riverbank. The gharial is much faster than his great lumbering cousins, thanks to his thin snout, which cuts through the water like an oar on its side. The male has a pot or *ghara* at the end of the snout that grows with maturity. It is used to make hissing noises and to blow bubbles that the lady crocs apparently find quite delightful. Rather unforgettable, we're sure you'll agree.

The crocodilians were once much more diverse than those we know now. There were dog-like crocodiles that would gallop after dinosaurs for brunch, and rat-like ones that would crunch on bugs. The most infamous has to be Deinosuchus—a terrifying specimen the size of a train carriage.

"NO, REALLY, I DON'T MIND IF YOU STAND THERE AT ALL."

The jaws of *Deinosuchus* would have been big enough to stand in, though that would have been a very silly place to stand.

Gharials live in three oddly shaped splodges over Bangladesh, Bhutan, and India.

TEXAS HORNED LIZARD

PHRYNOSOMA CORNUTUM

This horny beast … apologies, that sort of rude language won't do, will it? This spiky fellow has evolved to become the most disgusting meal ever. At least, the most disgusting meal since we had the haggis. Say "How do you do?" to the Texas horned lizard.

This frightful chap is the biggest and most widespread lizard in the United States, where he eats lots and lots of ants, with a side of locusts, and perhaps a little beetle for dessert if he feels he has been a good lizard. He likes a drink, too—don't we all—and when a rainstorm comes in he shoves his bottom in the air and allows the water to drizzle down his back to the corner of his mouth. How very refreshing.

As we have already intimated, it is his aversion to getting eaten that propels this scaly gent into this book. Of course, most animals have an inclination towards not being torn into tiny fleshy pieces by some beast that outsizes them by ten to one, and quite naturally there have been many evolutionary advancements toward avoiding just such a sticky end. In the case of the Texas horned lizard, when it comes to a crunch he stands stock-still. Not the best option, you would think, but then this wry fellow has a trick or two up his sleeve. He stands stock-still for a reason, you see—those horny parts make for rather good camouflage. If he is spotted he makes the rather unexpected move of shooting blood out of his eyes. A startling enough maneuver in its own right, you might say, but in addition the blood is said to taste foul to coyotes.

"DON'T COME ANY CLOSER OR I'LL BLOODY DO IT."

Something in Your Eye?

Now blood, as I am sure you're aware, is not a substance known for its shooting-out-of-your-eye-i-ness, which makes the Texas horned lizard's behavior a surprising sight to behold. Not only is it a remarkable spectacle, it rather neatly demonstrates an important aspect of evolution, namely that evolution only has a set number of materials to work with. The flipper that helped some forward-thinking fish out of the ocean has, over an excruciatingly long period of time, developed into all sorts of wonderful things—legs

Vestigial structures

For every marvelous body part that has become essential for survival, there are others that have become obsolete. These "vestigial structures," as they are known, are still somewhere inside the body's innards, although they can be minute. Snakes have pelvises, as do whales; manatees have toenails; flightless birds still have wings. We jumped-up primates, of course, have quite a few useless bits, too: we get goose bumps from little muscles that would have been used to raise a nice warm blanket of primate fur for us; we have an appendix that would have been much bigger and able to digest primate foods; we even have a little primate tail. These are fine examples of why "intelligent design" is utter piffle, of course, as why would a deity design the imperfect?

> A Texas horned lizard that has just squirted out some of its red stuff in an attempt to repel a peckish predator.

"I WOULDN'T TRY TO EAT ME OLD BEAN,
I'M RATHER ON THE RARE SIDE."

and claws, hands and wings, and sometimes even back into flippers again. The tiny bones that make up our ears were once simple parts of the jaw. Something as wondrous as a lady's bosom was once little more than a jumped-up sweat gland. All animals are made up of much the same bits and pieces, almost as if the bits and pieces are rubber bands that can be stretched and pulled in different directions to accomplish different things. Thus, evolution has a blueprint, and the Texas horned lizard has quite naturally evolved to shoot toxic blood out of his eyes if you try and make a meal out of him.

> A number of other states are lucky enough to have the Texas horned lizard, though he does tend to go on a bit about how great it was back in the Lone Star State.

A Hard Mouthful to Swallow

As mentioned, the Texas horned lizard likes an ant or two for brunch, and therein lies a problem. His favored lunch is the harvester ant, which is sadly being forced out of its neighborhood by the recently introduced and spectacularly unfriendly fire ant (pp. 54–5) from South America. Now the Texas horned lizard has tried this trendy new foreign food, and quite frankly it is a little rich for his blood, so his food source is diminishing. What is more, the pesticides used to get rid of the fire ants aren't doing much for the lizard either. So it seems this rather disgusting meal is being pushed off the face of the earth by another rather disgusting meal.

KOMODO DRAGON
VARANUS KOMODOENSIS

This is the story of an island giant. No, not King Kong, or even Godzilla for that matter. Huddle up, dear reader, as we hear a tale every bit as incredible and discover a monster every bit as abominable . . .

In 1492, a German navigator called Martin Behaim covered a metal ball with a map and thought it rather splendid. He called it the *Erdapfel* (literally "earth apple"), and though it lacked the Americas and even had a few made-up countries for good measure, it was the first globe. The second-oldest globe is of an unknown origin; the Hunt-Lenox globe, as it is known, is dated variously between 1503 and 1510, and is emblazoned with a really rather smashing description across Asia: *Hic sunt dracones* ("Here be dragons"). Remarkably, given the fame of this phrase, it is the only time that such an inscription appeared on any surviving antiquated map. Even more remarkably, it turned out to be right; there were indeed dragons ... it just took us a while to find them.

Landing in Trouble

In 1908, a pioneering Dutch aviator crash-landed into shark-infested waters in a far-flung corner of the East Indies. He thought himself the luckiest chap alive, as he had managed to cheat certain death, but he quickly rethought his position when he found himself shacked up on an island with slobbering ten-foot (3-m)-long man-eating lizards. Somehow our Dutch friend escaped this devilish pickle and on his return three months later, he told everyone he knew about his incredible escapades on the island of the dragons. Unfortunately, it was presumably commonplace for people in the Nether-

The Komodo dragon: a ten-foot-long lizard with terrible table manners.

Komodo dragons don't just live on the island of Komodo; they are adept swimmers and so can be found on neighboring islands such as Rinca and Flores where the natives are no doubt delighted to find them on their doorstep.

"WHAT DO YOU MEAN, I NEVER LEAVE A TABLE UNTIL EVERYONE'S EATEN?"

LEXICON

Island Gigantism

Large mammalian predators don't do frightfully well on piddly little islands due to a lack of space in which to roam. This means that birds and reptiles on islands may take their place and grow to monstrous proportions: a phenomenon known to biologists as "island gigantism." Conversely, large animals may become smaller on islands, a process known as insular dwarfism (see p. 117).

A It would take more than this to persuade a Komodo dragon not to eat you.

lands to hallucinate fantastical creatures most days of the week, because everyone thought he was talking nonsense.

Years after our hapless Dutch friend crashed, the skin and bones of a Komodo dragon made it to the island of Java, where a learned type wrote a paper about them, though it wasn't until 1926 that the world-famous explorer W. Douglas Burden proposed an expedition to catch a glimpse of the magnificent beasts. Unfortunately for the Komodos, in those times "catching a glimpse" generally translated to "filling them with lead pellets." Thankfully, some of the dragons were lucky, and W. Douglas Burden took a couple of live ones back to civilization.

Island Hopping

This massive lizard, like the rest of the monitor lizards, first evolved in Australia. Fifteen million years ago, Australia rather clumsily bumped into Southeast Asia, sloshing some of its native monitor lizards onto the islands there. On one of the tiny islands, Komodo, the lizards were subject to those tricky laws of evolution, and became an example of island gigantism (see box). What's more, they have a great big mouth full of nasty bugs that means if you are unlucky enough to get bitten by the swine, you'll slowly succumb to blood poisoning. Recently, it has been found that Komodo dragons have venom glands in the lower jaw. The poison causes shock and general wooziness—as if shock and wooziness were needed when you have just been bitten by a ten-foot lizard.

All big, horrible, man-eating lizards can have a sweet side, though, and it turns out these dragons are actually remarkably intelligent. Not a very lovable trait in an enormous venomous man-eating lizard, you'd think, but they like to play. In captivity they even recognize their individual keepers and can be taught to do tricks. Unlike a certain King Kong—a film, incidentally that was inspired by a gentleman called W. Douglas Burden and his expedition to Komodo Island.

Fact

Komodo dragons wouldn't think twice about gobbling you up, and these brutes genuinely are man-eaters—they've killed five people in the last 30 years alone. These devilish cads will even stoop to a bit of cannibalism: ten percent of their diet is young Komodos, who not surprisingly have decided to live in trees. While eating babies—even if you are really hungry—is frowned upon in most societies, it is necessary for these dragons as there are few medium-sized prey on the islands.

CHAPTER

5

BIRDS

Millions of years ago, some scaly fiends known as the dinosaurs were busy stomping around a big wet rock. One or two decided that all this lumbering was really rather boring and developed warm blood to help them move fast. Others thought the weather was quite frankly not to their liking and so they evolved a new fuzzy coat.

These feathered dinosaurs soon discovered that their feathers were all sorts of fun; they could use them to look nice and make all sorts of interesting shapes. Eventually the feathers became big enough to help their owners hop over things, and soon enough they could even use them to fly.

When a meteor struck our wet rock, the dinosaurs were wiped out and the survivors began filling all the little holes. They swooped in the skies, sploshed through the seas, and even stomped around like big feathery fiends.

STORK

FAMILY: CICONIIDAE

Storks are marvelous fellows that are famed for appearing out of nowhere every year. Surprisingly, no one could work out where they came from until one of them turned up with a bit more than a crick in his neck.

Storks are magnificent birds: huge and dignified, yet as quiet as a mouse. The stork lacks a syrinx—the part that allows a bird to sing—and so is one of the few mute birds. No surprise, then, that this chap kept the biggest secret in the avian kingdom for thousands of years.

They are often credited as being the bringer of babies. Fear not, however, I'm not about to go on one of my famed rants about debauchery and our slide into sinful-

Fact

Inspired by the stork, Otto Lilienthal's (1848–1896) gliders were major inspirations for the Wright brothers. He studied the stork, then went to technical college, studied the stork again, before finally building some rather marvelous gliders to lift himself off steep hills with. Otto's final flight took place in 1896; after losing lift at an altitude of 55 feet (17 m), he broke his spine and died in Berlin the following day. His final words were "Kleine Opfer müssen gebracht werden!" or "Small sacrifices must be made!"

> As the stork does not have a syrinx, he instead clacks his bill together as an alternative means of communication.

"ACTUALLY, I'VE CHANGED MY MIND."

"I SHALL MAINTAIN A DIGNIFIED SILENCE."

ness. Rather, storks are thought of in this manner because in times past they had a reputation for appearing in Europe out of the blue. Here they would mate, have their young, act like a delightful couple, become quite the talk of town, watch the little one grow, teach him about the birds and the bees, watch him fly the nest ... and promptly disappear again. In time, the stork became associated with the arrival of good fortune. Later, stuffy Victorians would use the bird as a foil to explain to young Timmy where babies come from. It was this rather remarkable habit the European stork had of disappearing each winter that flummoxed early naturalists. Until, that is, a rather unfortunate gentleman arrived in Germany in 1822.

Storks are real jetsetters, turning up in all sorts of places around the planet.

Known as the *Pfeilstorch*, or "arrow stork" in a more civilized tongue, this creature had arrived with an arrow in its neck. What is more, that arrow was of African origin, and so learned types surmised that birds travel great distances with the seasons ... in a word, they migrate. Previous ideas about their sudden disappearance over winter included that they turned into mice, or that they all went for a nap at the bottom of the sea.

Fact

"I NEVER COULD GET THE HANG OF LIGHTING MY PIPE ON THE STOVE."

The marabou stork, or undertaker bird, is the largest of the stork family, with some growing up to five feet (1.5 m) tall. His wing span can match that of the largest flying bird, the great Andean condor. It is not surprising he's called the undertaker bird either; the marabou stork is a gruesome-looking bird that appears to be wearing the feathered version of an undertaker's garb, and spends most of his day disposing of carrion on the African plains. The marabou stork also has a habit of going to the toilet all over his legs, though that is probably where the undertaker analogy ends.

The marabou stork is really quite ghastly. He can often be found scavenging around waste sites for scraps of food, which makes rats seem positively delightful by comparison.

LONG-TAILED WIDOW BIRD

EUPLECTES PROGNE

The long-tailed widow bird has a monstrous appendage that girls find rather delightful! Ah yes, quite ... I suppose its name has rather given away the punchline ... this fellow has a big tail that is a hit with the ladies.

The long-tailed widow bird lives in southern Africa on grassy plains. It is about the size of a sparrow, with an incredible two-foot (60-cm)-long tail trailing behind him to impress the female long-tailed widow birds. Just to put that into perspective, that would be the same as you or me dragging along a speedboat to a date ... which would no doubt impress the young lady you are courting, though I would warrant your fellow diners would be less than impressed.

These well-endowed male birds have evolved their fabulous tails through sexual selection and like to show off their monstrous append-ages by flying and dancing over the grasslands in which they live.

Though it is not all this showing off that bobs these splendid birds under the scrutinizing eyes of us at The Pro-ceedings. It is the rather drab short-tailed females that we find fascinating, as it is they who are pulling the strings of the tricksy laws of evolution. If they like what they see they will agree to meet for a bit of a romp, and it is this so-called "female choice" that is the rather splendid evolutionary force at work.

The long-tailed widow bird displaying his magnificent appendage.

> Darwin believed that sexual selection was at work in humans and that beard length was one such display of fitness.

"AS WELL AS COMING UP WITH THE GREATEST IDEA MAN HAS EVER HAD, I AM ALSO A MAGNIFICENT LOVER."

You can never have enough ladies ... no really, there simply are not enough of them. They invest a lot of time into making babies and chaps simply can't get enough of them. The males, given unlimited females, an afternoon, and some sort of soothing lotion, could father a sizeable family. What's more, given some scientific apparatus and perhaps some racy etchings, one could knock out a few hundred million baby-makers in a minute and if you had the capacity, and of course were of a rather persuasive nature, it would be feasible to impregnate every single female member of a rather large country ... though Christmas would be quite hellish.

A Bird in the Hand

The females on the other hand invest time and effort in caring for their offspring. They start with a large energy-rich egg. If the parents are of a fun-loving and progressive species, the egg may be fertilized inside the female's body. After fertilization, while Dad is off on some noble pursuit, Junior is being fed and nourished and being kept all nice and warm in Mum's tum. To summarize, the father can have loads of babies, whereas the mother can have only a few, so it is in mum's interest to pick the best possible father. In a word: female choice. Damn ... in two words: female choice.

In the male long-tailed widow bird's case he shows just how attractive he is by showing off his great big tail. It can even be demonstrated that if you stick extra bits onto the male's tail the ladies find him even more delightful and no doubt offer him all sorts of extra fun! Of course, the process is a snowball effect: the gents with the big tails get more ladies, the ladies have bigger-tailed babies ... the process only stopping when the tail gets too big to fly, or the male with the most resplendent tail is always getting eaten.

(LEXICON)

Sexual selection

Sexual selection is a theory proposed by Charlie Darwin as to how certain evolutionary traits appear. There are a number of aspects to the theory, which has evolved itself over the years. Males kicking the hell out of each other—or "male–male competition" (see the hooded seal, pp. 136–7); ladies coyly pointing and giggling about which fellow they'd most like to take them down the aisle—or "female choice" (above); and other altogether more tricksy things going on like "sperm competition" (see the right whale, pp. 146–7).

This rather well-endowed bird can be found at the bottom of Africa.

JUNGLE FOWL

GALLUS SPP.

—⁘—

Red and gray jungle fowl are rather dashing tropical pheasants that dwell in the jungles of southeast Asia. Though you might find them more recognizable when they are naked, they are actually the direct ancestors of an altogether more familiar and rather intriguing old bird: the chicken.

The chicken is a bundle of tastiness that was borne from the interbreeding of these two jungle birds. Now, enough philosophizing; what of this omnipresent former jungle fowl, the chicken? We've seen plenty of fat birds with the deliciousness gene eaten off the planet, from the dodo to the great auk via the passenger pigeon and the kakapo. Though sometimes it works the other way round: we like the species so much we domesticate it, look after it, and reproduce it in incredible numbers—24 billion in the case of chickens, making it the most abundant bird on the planet … an incredible triumph in evolutionary terms. These delightful creatures also menstruate in handy little packages, and we find these little eggy periods absolutely delicious too! Sounds like something only your dog would eat, we know, but we manage to get through 69 billion a year … no, not just us two … we mean mankind. We like to have them boiled, with toast cut up into points.

"But what of that fabulous bird the jungle fowl?! This is all about chickens!" I hear you cry. Well, the fowl are smashing creatures, but are sadly nothing to write home about, though I can tell you they do taste a bit like chicken.

Fact

A chicken is the only animal to have lived without its head. In 1940s Colorado, things didn't look too rosy for Mike the chicken as he was due for the chop. Out came the axe, and off came his head, but Mike continued to live sans tête. It seems when the farmer lopped off his thinker, he'd kept the tiny bit of his brain that deals with breathing and whatnot. Mike lived for a further 18 months, becoming quite the star, and appearing in both Time *and* Life *magazines.*

▼ The gray jungle fowl frequents much of India, whereas the red jungle fowl has set up shop from the foothills of the Himalayas right through China and southeast Asia.

CASSOWARY

CASUARIUS SPP.

———❧———

The dinosaurs never truly went extinct. Extraordinary, we know, but they never died out—they just changed address and put on a disguise. The most fearsome dinosaurs, the theropods—which included the Tyrannosaurus rex—are still among us. Incredibly, birds are now classified as theropods, and of these the cassowary is undoubtedly the most dangerous.

Fact

Learned types originally thought that the dinosaurs were shambling lizards running around like today's cold-blooded scaly things. That was until someone discovered a chap called *Deinonychus*, who had to have been different. His skeleton revealed him to be a hunter that must have hurtled around and jumped on prey, killing by slashing and stabbing with his scythe-clawed back feet. Such an active lifestyle could only be achieved by having warm blood … the dinosaurs must have been more like birds than lizards.

The bird that their formidable ancestors would be most proud of has to be the cassowary. A tremendous beast it is, too: its kick can break bones, it can jump five feet (1.5 m) into the air, all the while brandishing its second toe, a 5-inch (12-cm)-long claw that is more like a dagger. Though, here at The Proceedings we feel it pertinent to report that the cassowary is not all bad. It turns out that, amid all the hyperbole and hullabaloo, only one human death has been attributed to a cassowary—a young boy who was hitting it with a stick at the time. The moral of the story: if you come across the closest thing you can find to a *Tyrannosaurus rex*, don't hit it with a stick.

Incidentally, the cassowary was not the most fearsome bird that ever lived. That title must go to the rather delightful-sounding "terror birds" that took over from the predatory dinosaurs when they decided they didn't like the planet after all. You really wouldn't want to mess with this fiend—it was about nine feet (2.75 m) tall and it ate horses. Thankfully, this particular beaky bastard is not with us any more.

"Just remember who's at the top of the pecking order, sunshine!"

The cassowary is best not to be found in Guinea and Australia.

VAMPIRE FINCH

GEOSPIZA DIFFICILIS SEPTENTRIONALIS

As Charlie Darwin sailed around the planet on the Beagle, *he was really rather taken by a number of birds, none more so than a group of songbirds from the Galápagos. It wasn't until the great man was back in Blighty that he realized they were all in fact finches … never mind the cornerstone of his mighty theory.*

Hidden in among "Darwin's finches" was a little devil that is easy to overlook, though it would be very hard to be taken by the little horror: the vampire finch. Years before the *Beagle*'s arrival, one or two finches had made the islands their home. From these beginnings they had adapted and evolved to exploit all the different opportunities that the Galápagos islands presented, with the vampire finch of course filling the ecological niche of resident "evil bastard."

The vampire finch is a subspecies of the sharp-beaked ground finch, and evolved on two of the smaller Galápagos islands—Darwin and Wolf. They are really rather arid little islands and so the finches learned to seek out moisture-rich foods. The finches nibble at succulent cacti and when they are big and strong enough will even peck at other bird's eggs. Younger vampire finches have worked out that they can roll the eggs off rocky ledges for a scrambled-egg surprise. Smashing other birds' eggs, however, apparently isn't quite nasty enough for some vampire finches. These swine will wait until the young chicks are hatched, before plucking out the newborns' little feathers and gobbling him down—like stealing candies from a baby. Stealing fancies from a fledgling, it seems, still doesn't satisfy their evil streak, though don't expect applause for working out where this horrific bird gets another meal. Quite, yes … they rather ghoulishly peck at the backs of the nesting booby population (see pp. 126–7) and slurp upon their blood. Strangely, the boobies don't seem to mind; it is thought that they think it normal for small birds to come and peck them for parasites. It could of course be that the boobies are insufferable imbeciles. Although the vampire finch is about as popular as Adolf is for a first name, it must be said that they are simply trying to survive.

"A VAMPIRE! QUICK, SHOW HIM YOUR CROSS!" … "VERY WELL. STOP PECKING ME YOU LITTLE BASTARD!!"

The large ground finch has a big beak that he uses to crack nuts.

The vampire finch is only found on two minuscule islands in the Galápagos, much to the relief of the booby population.

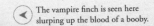

The vampire finch is seen here slurping up the blood of a booby.

BEE HUMMINGBIRD

MELLISUGA HELENAE

Native to Cuba, the zunzuncito, *or bee hummingbird, is the teeniest, tiniest bird in the world. At only two inches (5 cm) long he is not much bigger than a bee and weighs in at just slightly heavier than a paperclip. What's more, the tiny chap is never far from death.*

The bee hummingbird's nest is like a boiled egg chopped in half, just without the goo. Its own eggs are unsurprisingly teensy weensy—the size of a coffee bean, though not as good for breakfast. These tiny birds beat their wings at a remarkable 80 times per second, though when they are mating they really go at it hammer and tongs with 200 beats a second.

The bird's minuscule heart beats at up to an incredible 1,200 times a minute. What's more he can take as many as 500 breaths in that time. Not surprisingly he has the highest metabolic rate of any animal—they need to convert food into energy very quickly, and for this very reason they are constantly feeding.

They are rather busy in their day-to-day affairs, having to visit around 1,500 flowers a day for the nectar, which they suck up with their straw-like tongue, though they do also inhale the odd insect when the mood takes them. The food is processed within minutes, there being not enough room in the bird's tiny body for grub to sit around undigested. What's more, they take in a terrific amount of calories; if we were as busy as the bee hummingbird we'd need to eat about 70 times more food than we actually do.

After they've kissed their tiny ones goodnight, put out the tiny cat, and put on their miniature pajamas, they enter a state more like hibernation than sleep to conserve energy. At daybreak there is no time to brush their tiny teeth, even if they had them, because as soon as they wake they must find food or risk starving to death.

The bee hummingbird is found solely on the island of Cuba, and then you have to look very carefully for it.

The male bee hummingbird ... only a teeny bit bigger than this picture.

LEXICON

Insular Dwarfism

This is the process and condition of turning tiny, usually on an island. There are a number of theories as to why it might exist, including the idea that the relative scarcity of food on islands places smaller individuals at a distinct advantage. Examples include the tiny Honshu wolf of Japan, the recent itty, bitty human remains found on the island of Flores, and of course the rather tiny bee hummingbird of Cuba.

Fact

The largest bird on the planet is the flightless ostrich, which can be up to nine feet (2.75 m) tall. The largest flying bird is the mighty Andean condor that has a wingspan up to ten feet (3 m) across.

SUPERB LYREBIRD

MENURA NOVAEHOLLANDIAE

This is the superb lyrebird ... no, that really is his name, though it's fair to say this bird really is superb. They did toy around with calling it the smashing lyrebird and the Why, Isn't He Just Delightful! Lyrebird, but "superb lyrebird" stuck. The only other species of lyrebird, the Albert's lyrebird, is said to be really rather jealous of this grand moniker.

Lyrebirds are pheasant-sized birds that hurtle around the Australian rainforest floor. What's more, it seems they really like it down there, as they are a bit awkward in the air. Any sign of danger and they will dash straight down the nearest wombat hole—if they can find one. Although it is not the ability to run away that has propelled these superb (yes, I am including you under that heading, Albert, so do stop sulking) creatures into the book. In fact, what is ever so strange about these chaps is their quite frankly incredible mating rituals.

The male lyrebird will begin his tomfoolery in winter when he builds and maintains a mound to perform on. The lyrebirds have the most complicated syrinx (see p. 111) of the songbirds, which means this incredible fellow can sing the most beautiful songs. What is more, they can mimic just about any sound they hear.

Passerines

Passerines, often quite wrongly referred to as the songbirds, are quite rightly referred to as the perching birds, though they are quite often songbirds ... in case that makes any sense.

"Look at it dear, they've stuck it on the wrong way. It looks ridiculous."

When John Gould painted this, it was from a specimen that had been shot and carted around the planet—presumably rather roughly as the male's tail is on the wrong way around.

"... JUST A CITY BOY, BORN AND RAISED IN SOUTH DETROIT ..."

LEXICON

Cloaca

Birds, along with amphibians, the monotremes, and some fish, lack separate reproductive and intestinal openings. Put simply, they do all their business through the same hole, the cloaca. A bird may ravish a female in a matter of seconds by the coming together of their cloacae, known as a "cloacal kiss." With all the whatnot that goes on down there, we can understand why they do it so quickly.

In the 1930s, a lyrebird by the name of James formed a bond with a lady called Mrs. Wilkinson. After she had fed him over a number of years he returned the favor by performing his courtship dance in her garden, even when she had guests, although only if she was present. The word "dance" of course is perhaps a misnomer, as it is really the song that is the highlight of the performance. James was said to include in his song the sounds of ... the laughing song of the kookaburra, two kookaburras having a laugh together, an Australian magpie and a young magpie begging for food, a bellbird, an eastern whipbird—I say, I like the sound of her—a yellow-tailed black cockatoo, a gang-gang cockatoo, an Eastern rosella, a pied butcherbird, a wattlebird, a gray shrike-thrush, a thornbill, a white-browed scrubwren, a striated pardalote, a starling, a yellow robin, a golden whistler, a flock of parrots having a merry old time, a crimson rosella, several other birds that no one could identify, the faintissimo cheeps of thousands of honeyeaters ... a rock pulverizer, a hydraulic ram, and the tooting of motorcar horns!

Really rather amazing, isn't it? Once a park ranger went bushwhacking to find out why the blazes someone was playing a merry ditty on a flute in the middle of the bush. Turns out that the culprit was a lyrebird who had learned the tunes from a nearby farm where they had a gramophone for shindigs. I would of course be very happy to go on about this marvelous fellow, but I am really the last person who should lecture on the subject of making good impressions.

This lyrebird can be found being superb in the forests of southeastern Australia and south Tasmania.

TAWNY FROGMOUTH

PODARGUS STRIGOIDES

❦

Say hello to this rather fantastic bird. He may look like an owl, but to all intents and purposes the tawny frogmouth has evolved into a feathered trashcan.

Hmmm … this feathery wonder lives in Australia, including Tasmania, and there are a few in southern New Guinea. Yes, we know he looks like an owl but he is actually more closely related to the nightjars and oilbirds. Old frog-features sits in the forest at night and, well, just sits there, waiting for insects to buzz by. If an insect is unlucky enough to bob past this big feathery frog-mouthed trashcan they quickly wish they hadn't. The tawny frogmouth is a "sit and wait" predator—a bit like a kingfisher sitting on a riverbank, though he is not about to get wet. Those wispy, whiskery feathers around his mouth are thought to detect anything that would rather not be chomped on … and help the tawny frogmouth to quickly go about ruining their day by chomping on them. Yes, we know, owls eat things in the night too, but owls go about their nighttime dining quite differently. They scour large areas looking for prey to skewer with their rather vicious-looking feet, rather than sit on a branch waiting for something to wander past their enormous mouth.

The tawny frogmouth's camouflage is tip-top and he exhibits a behavior known as "stumping"—though referring to "looking like a tree stump" as a behavior is probably a misnomer. As it turns out, doing nothing is generally a rather good way of not getting seen; predators on the whole are on the look out for things that … well, move around. Again, this is where owls differ from our friend as they are renowned for doing things like flying about, hunting mice, and hooting and hollering.

▼ The tawny frogmouth and his rather magnificent maw.

"3... 2... 1... COMING, READY OR NOT!"

Owls often make a din, generally because they are renowned imbeciles due to the fact that their huge eyes leave very little space for the gray stuff. What is more, a big slice of their tiny minds is devoted to processing the huge amounts of information their incredible eyes and ears pick up. Aaaah finally, yes, something very owl-like about the tawny frogmouth ... he is an utter buffoon. Recently, frogmouths have noticed that insects are attracted to those newfangled electric lamps ... the problem being that electric lamps are more often than not attached to the front of motor cars. Such a *kamikaze* behavior is surely about to become a rather quick lesson in survival of the fittest for these silly fellows.

The tawny frogmouth can be found in Australia, Tasmania, and southern New Guinea. Or at least he can if he's not playing silly buggers and pretending to be a stump again.

(LEXICON)

Crypsis

Animals tend to avoid being too conspicuous, which is why you rarely see them indulging in heated telephone conversations in the library. Being overly visible tends to get them into the belly of something bigger than them and so our animal chums have worked out all sorts of clever ways of not being visible. This is what we call *crypsis*. Of course, camouflage is one method, and the tawny frogmouth is an expert in this field; its feathers look exactly like tree bark. There are many other ways in which an animal may try to remain unseen or in a state of crypsis, including only coming out at night, living underground, or even being see-through.

ADÉLIE PENGUIN

PYGOSCELIS ADELIAE

❦

It was the intrepid French explorer and naval type Jules Sébastien César Dumont d'Urville who first set eyes on a rather sweet and diminutive penguin, which he promptly named after his wife, Adélie. Sadly for Dumont, this rather romantic gesture lost some of its allure after it became apparent that the female Adélie penguin was in fact a trollop.

"Brazen strumpetry!"

The Adélie penguins live on the Antarctic beaches, where the weather can be awfully variable. These naughty little fellows are thankfully a resourceful bunch and have found a way of keeping their seed in good shape by building stony nests to protect their eggs against the elements. These stones are not that plentiful, so there are some mighty squabbles over them. The stronger males eventually take the most pebbles and build the best nests. When the female Adélies return from the better part of a year at sea, they will choose a mate and soon steer toward the strong provider penguin who has proved himself by building up a good tall nest.

That is not, dear reader, the end of the story. As we have said, the female Adélie penguin is quite the strumpet. It seems that as soon as hubby's back is turned she is getting rather loose with the neighbors—those males who haven't had any success at finding a mate. In return for a frolic with her, the bachelor penguins are rather happy to pay … the princely sum of one pebble. In fact, some of the more ambitious female Adélies have been observed prostituting themselves over 62 times in a breeding season. Of course there is no record of Jules Sébastien César Dumont d'Urville's wife Adélie Dumont being anything like her penguin namesakes.

Ⓐ The Adélie penguin wasn't the only thing that d'Urville discovered. He also found the famous Venus de Milo statue in the ownership of a Greek peasant.

Fact

There are of course a number of animals that pay in some way or other for sex. Chimps will barter meat and macaques will groom for it. Purple-throated Carib hummingbirds will allow females to come and eat around their place for a quickie. The male dance fly goes a step further and wraps up his present for her; she'll unwrap the gift only to find that it's empty, allowing the male enough time to have his wicked way.

⟩ If you are visiting Adélie, do remember to bring along a few pebbles; it might just keep her off the mean streets.

TOCO TOUCAN

RAMPHASTOS TOCO

The Toco toucan lives in South America, where he shuttles around through the trees eating fruit. His beak is the largest in the avian kingdom, at least compared to the size of the bird; in fact it makes up to 50 percent of his body surface area. Though why this is so is something of a mystery.

This chap obviously has a rather large hooter, and we just can't help but be drawn to it. French naturalist Georges-Louis Leclerc, Comte de Buffon, described it as a "grossly monstrous" appendage. Darwin hypothesized that "toucans may owe the enormous size of their beaks to sexual selection, for the sake of displaying the diversified and vivid stripes of color with which these organs are ornamented." Quite right, too; a number of big colorful appendages can be attributed to wooing the fairer sex, as with the long-tailed widow bird (pp. 112–3).

Other suggestions as to why this amazing creature has such a hooter include for use as a fruit peeler, to intimidate little birds, and as a visual warning. A good suggestion was that it had evolved a bit like a giraffe's neck, and indeed it is handy for reaching those hard-to-get fruits. Then, just the other year, someone made a remarkable discovery. When an infrared camera is pointed at the Toco toucan's beak it glows like a red-hot poker! One of the major functions of his mighty beak is that it is a heat-exchange system, like an elephant's ear. It is used like a radiator to cool him down when he's in a bit of a flap. Indeed, the big schnoz's capacity to lose heat is comparable to Dumbo's flappers. It goes a little way to explaining why the Toco toucan sleeps with his beak all nice and warm tucked up under his wing.

The Toco toucan is found dotted around South America. You can't miss him; he's that beaky chap, remember.

Fact

The reasons why the Toco toucan has such an enormous schnoz are multiple. Indeed, there are some rather famous examples of adaptations that are more significant than first meets the eye—not least the giraffe's neck. Most people associate it with being able to reach leaves at the tops of trees, though giraffes also use their necks to fight by banging their heads into each other's body, and so the long neck aids in fisticuffs.

"IT'S A BLOODY BEAK, I USE IT TO EAT WITH!"

A Toco toucan. If you look very carefully you might just spot his beak.

KAKAPO

STRIGOPS HABROPTILA

The world's fattest and only flightless parrot is an adorable tubby lump whose memoirs read like a pamphlet on how to get eaten. Short of evolving a coating of herb butter, and having a nest like a Savoy fricassée with a little beetroot-relish quinelle egg, the rather marvelous kakapo has seemingly gone out of his way to become a somewhat easy meal. So easy, in fact, that there are only a hundred or so left.

The kakapo lives on a couple of tiny islands at the bottom of New Zealand. Of course, New Zealand was one of the last countries to be discovered by man. Bird life flourished here and evolved to fill all those little niches usually filled by mammals. Unmolested by big predators, the birds forwent the ability to fly and instead waddled around the forest floor happily chomping on the nuts, berries, and fruit that would usually be eaten by pigs, mice, and deer. Chomping on quite a lot of it, in the case of the chubby kakapo.

Eventually, man arrived. By now he had had ample time to demonstrate that he is not the nicest of guests, most unlikely to bring any chocolates. True to form, he instead brought horrid things that really weren't to the kakapos' liking. The kakapo was the third most common bird on New Zealand before man arrived. Being delicious is not the best adaptation that evolution has ever produced, however, and so this was quick to change. The Maori and their pooches devoured them. Kakapo smell worse than a bar carpet on a Sunday morning, and so were a tad easy to find. What's more, their response to danger is to stand stock-still—petrified, as it were. To make matters even worse, the next wave of invaders brought pigs, goats, deer, and horses—all of which loved to eat the same things as the kakapo.

"Are you stuck? I told you not to have that second helping of dessert."

These fat parrots are found on a remote island off New Zealand. If there is a less salubrious address, the author is unaware of it.

A Fruity Sort

Now, many birds throughout history have evolved the deliciousness gene and quite a few of these have been eaten off the planet: the dodo, the passenger pigeon, and the great auk, to name but a few. So here at the Proceedings we only allow an entry if it displays an added *soupçon* of the strange. Thankfully, the kakapo delivers in droves.

You see, this rotund fellow has rather bizarre breeding behavior. The kakapo will only breed in certain years when a particular type of fruit abounds. If it does happen to be one of these years, kakapo males will waddle up to ridges where they will begin to fight, sometimes to the death, for the best spots. Once a spot is secured, the male will go and tidy up the saucer-shaped bowls formed by year upon year of rooting around. One way that researchers find out if a bowl is in use is by popping a few twigs in it—if it's used overnight, they'll have been removed by the morning. Once in their immaculate bowls, the kakapo make a booming noise to attract any females nearby to mate with, and they will continue to do so for about four months, losing half their body weight in the process. Not only that, they are very, very rampant—so in need of nuptials, in fact, that they've been observed mating with dead seabirds.

The Polynesians were also fond of rats to eat and really couldn't bear to be without them, so brought them to New Zealand. Sadly, the rats in turn were fond of the kakapo's eggs. Understandably, everyone gave up on the whole eating rats thing when they discovered all the delicious things New Zealand had to offer ... which in turn meant more rats to eat more eggs.

"*There goes the neighborhood.*"

This booming obviously attracts more than their scarce mates. Indeed, it would probably be safe to say that the kakapo's attempts at getting a lady into the sack are actually more efficient at bringing down the population numbers than adding to them. Thankfully, due to some rather brilliant research, and more than a dash of diligence, a group of learned types are helping to claw this fat parrot from the brink of extinction. From 40 pairs in the 1980s, there are now over 100 in the wild. Good show, chaps!

To summarize: if you are a tubby, delicious meal who can be smelled a mile off, and you are not really concentrating because you're so permanently ready for sex that you'd have it with a rotten seagull ... and you are loud ... and the new next-door neighbors are hungry Polynesians and their pets . . . and you can't fly away or actually make any kind of response to being attacked ... things aren't going to pan out too well for you.

BOOBY

SULA SPP.

Despite what you may or not have been thinking, we are of course talking about the rather enchanting seabird from the Pacific. Naturally, among sailors these affable birds were really rather popular. They would comically drop in to say "How do you do?" on ships that were mid-voyage. What sailor couldn't be taken in by this bird's comical looks, bold-as-brass personality, waddling gait ... and, of course, being a hell of a lot tastier than a biscuit full of weevils and a flask of your own urine can't have done their appeal any harm.

Though it is not for any of these reasons that this smasher is propelled into The Proceedings. It is actually because of its poop, and to be fair the poop of a couple of his pals: the Peruvian cormorant and the Peruvian pelican. A triumvirate of the most important ploppers the world has ever seen.

The Incas are of course famous for building cities of gold that are even more difficult to find than an honest lawyer. What is less lauded is their love of bird poop. The Inca revered the islands of fertilizer and anyone who disturbed the holy birds was subject to the death penalty. The Inca, in their native Quechua, referred to this white stinky gold as *wanu*. The Spanish, of course, not happy with merely oppressing the natives, felt they should also spray them with spittle, so changed the name to *guano*.

Fact

The most famous of the boobies—the blue-footed—are famous for their comical mating dance that involves waving around their enormous feet. The bluer the charming chap's feet, the more likely the female is to find him quite dashing.

*"WHATEVER YOU DO, LAY OFF O'
MAH BLUE WEBBED FEET."*

These silly fellows can be found in quite a swathe across the hemisphere.

Of course, it wasn't just the natives that thought the poop delightful. Step forward the great poop rush of the 1800s. Fortunes were born from the bottoms of seabirds. In 1858 alone Great Britain imported 300,000 tons of Peruvian guano, mainly for growing turnips. The British Empire pretty much ran the whole guano empire, rather annoying our American friends, and indeed it became United States law that if an American found an island full of bird poop, he was allowed to keep the entire island … as long as he sent all that poop back to the US.

Between 1840 and 1880, the Peruvian guano boom was at its height. Twenty million tons were exported, earning the country two billion dollars; indeed, the president of Peru was said to be more important than the president of the United States at the time. Sadly, he thought a windfall of two billion dollars not enough to bolster his country's coffers and promptly took out a number of crippling loans. Wars soon broke out over the precious poop, resulting in a number of bloody conflicts which culminated in poor blooming Bolivia being a landlocked country with an active navy. Nor was it just Bolivia that was left in a right bloody mess. It has been argued that many of South America's woes are because of this financial mismanagement of such a precious early resource. All of which, of course, that daft bugger the booby, and indeed his poop, are utterly oblivious to.

> Masked boobies are the biggest of the booby family, making them rather prone to immature jokes.

CHAPTER

6

MAMMALS

While the dinosaurs were stomping around, the mammals were getting all warm and fuzzy, skulking around trying to avoid becoming a hot meal, and biding their time until the big lizards bit the dust.

While they are an ever so diverse family, they do have something in common: they all give milk to their young. A smashing idea it is too, because it allows them to stay with their kids and make sure nothing tries to chomp on them.

Say "How do you do?" to your family—the ones that are all warm and fuzzy on the outside. They're a delightful bunch we are sure you'll agree … and rather prone to making you feel all warm and fuzzy on the inside.

PINK FAIRY ARMADILLO

CHLAMYPHORUS TRUNCATUS

The armadillos, or "little armored ones," are a jolly bunch of creatures mainly from the Americas. While the giant armadillo of the Brazilian rainforest looks like a huge armored knight, you can plop the pink fairy armadillo in the palm of your hand like an imp in full battle regalia. The armor is really rather tough too, made from bone with a covering of horn, making this fellow a knight resplendent enough for any fairy tale.

Fact

The nine-banded armadillo has a rather unusual defense mechanism: it jumps high into the air. Rather effective it was too, until the advent of the motorcar. Previously it had the chance to miss the wheels and remain relatively unscathed, but now of course it jumps slap bang into the middle of the radiator.

The pink fairy armadillo can be found not picking fights with big lizards, nor indeed molesting comatose royalty, but rather moving around the sandy plains of central Argentina.

Once upon a time there were the armadillos, who were mostly world-class skedaddlers, all except for a small pink fellow who was a champion swimmer. What's that, it doesn't merit an entry in this book? Well, I'll have you know that this smasher is quite the champion at swimming through solid rock. Oh OK, not through solid rock, but he can really shove his way through the tough stuff. The fairy-tale fellow is what is known as a sand swimmer; he sploshes around under the desert sands. What's more, he is rather good at it. The pink fairy armadillo can bury himself in seconds if threatened, like a diver plopping into a pool. He is built rather like a boat, his snout plowing a furrow through the sandy sea, and his head not surprisingly armored to make sure he doesn't rub the bloody thing off.

Our hero may also use that armor of his to stop any would-be diners, using it to block their burrow like a stopper in a bottle. Sadly, there seem to be plenty of animals that would like to gobble down these handsome heroes—big bad wolves to be exact … or at least domestic dogs. These fearsome hounds, along with encroaching farmland, mean that life may not be the fairy tale it promised for the pink fairy armadillo, as sadly they are becoming rather rare. Let's just hope it is not …

The End.

LEXICON

Leprosy

Aside from us humans, the armadillos are the only other creature that can catch the nasty disease leprosy. Leprosy does not directly cause body parts to plonk off the body willy-nilly; it is rather a bacteria that munches on the ends of your nerves, causing your skin to crinkle up and making it very hard to feel anything. Not feeling things results in constant injury, and if you don't manage to lose body parts, you may have to get them chopped off.

ST. KITTS VERVET MONKEY

CHLOROCEBUS SPP.

These lucky monkeys have the rather enviable ecological niche of hanging around in the Caribbean drinking cocktails.

Vervets, it seems, are on a bit of a jolly; they are mere tourists to the island paradise of St. Kitts. These monkeys originally came from Africa, imported as pets on the boats that brought over slaves to the Caribbean in the seventeenth century.

In the Caribbean the monkeys have flourished in the wild and have regularly caused chaos throughout the Antilles, none more so than the population on St. Kitts. You see the St. Kitts vervets have taken to boozing. Originally they found sugar cane fermenting on the local plantations, but now they've found a more ready source: tourists.

The troops of monkeys come out of the forests to the beach, where they admire girls and steal booze. Of course, everyone likes a drunk and everyone likes a monkey ... so what could be better? Though I think you know by now that drunkenness ... apart from in the case of the author ... isn't enough to get you into the Proceedings of the Ever so Strange.

Learned types have discovered that the vervets have rather human patterns of imbibing. How so? Well, the vast majority of them are social drinkers: they drink in moderation and only after midday. Fifteen percent are steady drinkers who like a more regular tipple, and another fifteen percent are teetotalers. Then there are the five percent who go at it like a sailor at a free bar, starting fights and often barely able to stand. Interestingly, it is the five percent who act up the most that become the dominant pack leaders. The author can think of nothing that equates to this in human society ... must try harder ... look like monkeys ... our leaders ... hmmm ... are drunks ... no sorry, still nothing.

Of course the vervets are remarkable fellows. As we hinted, they are rather partial to a tipple, but it is not the only reason they are a very welcome addition to The Proceedings. Put quite simply, their tallywhackers are a bright turquoise blue with a red bit on the end. The deeper the blue, the higher up the social ranking they lie.

"ALRIGHT, I KNOW I WAS RATHER TIPSY LAST NIGHT, BUT WHICH JOKER DID THIS TO ME?"

The St. Kitts vervet monkey is on his vacation on the Caribbean island of the same name. His folks back in Africa rarely receive a postcard ... though they are pleased that he is "having a nice time."

PYGMY HIPPOPOTAMUS

CHOEROPSIS LIBERIENSIS

Hippopotamuses. Tough is not the word; everyone knows them for their man-squashing temper tantrums, though few know that they are bulletproof and can move around on any terrain. Put quite simply, they have evolved into the biological equivalent of a tank. Then there is Choeropsis liberiensis, *the pygmy hippo … the anti-hippo.*

The hippo is renowned for its ferocity, and is often cited as the most dangerous animal in Africa. Of course, the mosquito is a far more dangerous animal than the hippo, though I know which one I'd rather tackle with a newspaper. While the hippo will think nothing of eating a boat or causing a ruckus through farms and villages, the pygmy hippo thinks all this rampaging quite tiresome, not least because he's knee-high and would be quite frankly abominable at the chore. He is a rather rare hippo from western Africa. *Hippopotamus* means "river horse" in Greek, and the locals call the pygmy hippo the "river pig," but the actual family tree of the hippos is a tad more smashing than that. Their closest living relatives are in fact the cetaceans— the whales and dolphins—which makes sense when you think about it really, a water-living fatso and all that.

If you are very lucky you might spot one of these cheeky chaps ambling around the bush in west Africa.

The pygmy hippopotamus comes quite far down the list of Africa's most fearsome creatures, which isn't surprising when you see them.

"No, I'm rather delightful company, to be honest."

Fact

A Sinking Feeling

Interestingly, despite spending 90 percent of their time in the water, hippos can't swim. To get around in the water they simply sink to the bottom of the river and trot along the bottom. The pygmy hippo spends a lot more time on dry land. To stop getting sunburn both types of hippo actually secrete sunscreen, or "blood sweat" as it has rather gruesomely become known. It is neither blood nor sweat, but instead a highly alkaline substance that turns pink in sunlight. It is also a rather effective antibacterial agent.

Pygmy hippos have a sloped back, which allows them to pass through the bush more effectively. They merrily mark their path by pooping, while in the process using their tiny tail to scatter the stuff all over. They are one of the few retromingent animals, meaning they urinate backwards. Of course, the point I'm very slowly getting round to is that the pygmy hippos are not chubby sociopaths with their heads full of blood lust. In fact, they are quite the opposite of the aggressive common hippo. They are adorable tubby lumps who are just begging for a scratch under the chin, although you'd be lucky to give the chap a tickle in the wild, not just because they are unfortunately very rare, but they are also shy and though no doubt they'd appreciate the tickle, they are quite frankly avoiding that big dangerous cousin of theirs.

(LEXICON)

Divergent evolution

Time and again we talk of convergent evolution (see tenrec, pp. 182–3), though it is divergent evolution that is perhaps the more familiar. It is the process of becoming more different, as in the case of a whale and a hippo.

The first whale was about as un-whaley as it gets. Current thinking is that the cetaceans, the whales and dolphins, evolved from fossils found in Pakistan, the pakicetids. Learned types know that they are whale ancestors from the bones of the ear and the lumps and bumps on the molar teeth. These pakicetids (below) were like weasely deer and spent much of their time around water about 15 million years ago.

There they evolved into the ambulocetids (below), also found in Pakistan deposits …

… which evolved into archaic whales, like the basilosaurs.

> Basilosaurs lived about 37 million years ago and were rather more brutish than the pygmy hippo. They were 60 feet (18 m) long and ate sharks as though they were mere fish sticks.

STAR-NOSED MOLE

CONDYLURA CRISTATA

Meet this marvelous mole and his rather splendid nose, which is said to be the most sensitive appendage in the entire animal kingdom.

The star-nosed mole lives in swamps in northern parts of North America and swims through the sloshy mud. A good swimmer, he is often found at the bottom of streams and ponds looking for food. It is fairly obvious what makes this chap a rather excellent entry in this book, though there is more to it than looking like he has inhaled a grenade.

Of course, these moles have eyes that are about as much use as a Turkish cricket team. In fact, they can only just perceive the difference between light and dark. Thankfully their magnificent hooter means that they don't really need to see; indeed if they were able, they would only see a blanket of mud, whereas their fleshy star-shaped nose is tremendously sensitive and will feel anything that wiggles by. What they don't feel they will certainly smell, even in water. Incredibly, the star-nosed mole is the only mammal that can smell underwater, a feat thought for a long time to be quite impossible. It does this by blowing large bubbles out of its nose and quickly snuffling them back up along with any smelly smells.

"I SAY, WHAT THE BLAZES IS GOING ON AROUND HERE?"

◄ Not only does the big starry nose sense touch, smell, and electricity, the tentacles also make sure it doesn't inhale food and mud.

(LEXICON)

Biomimicry

Nature has had millions of years to come up with some of the most remarkable feats of engineering. Not surprisingly we've started to emulate some of the most innovative critters— from trains that run smoother because their front is shaped like a bird's to buildings that are designed like termite mounds to allow natural air-conditioning. One new discipline in this novel science is the concept of self-assembling structures. As nothing in the world grows like a star-nosed mole's nose, who knows what amazing new feats will be inspired by it?

"SMELL YOU LATER, OLD BEAN."

No One Nose

So while it may be as blind as a bat-that-has-been-buried-in-a-swamp-with-a-big-distracting-nose-in-front-of-its-next-to-useless-eyes, the mole's stupendous nose more than makes up for that. It has 22 little pink fleshy tentacles like a flower. His superb schnoz is covered in incredibly sensitive organs called Eimer's organs—25,000 highly acute little nodules that relay information back to his brain. There are 100,000 nerves connecting his nose to his brain, which is six times as many as there are between the human brain and the hand. Which gives you an inkling as to just how much they can feel around a swamp. In fact it would be fair to say the star-nosed mole's nose is in fact his eyes; he even waves it around constantly, much like we gaze, looking for food, mates, pipe tobacco, and whatnot.

One more thing on this terrific creature. It turns out he is the fastest eater in the animal kingdom. In eight milliseconds he can figure out if something is food, and if it is indeed edible it will be slurped up within 120 milliseconds—three times faster than the blink of an eye.

You could try and sniff out a star-nosed mole in the swampy bits of the northeast Americas.

Everyone knows that we over-evolved apes have five senses: sight, hearing, touch, smell, and taste. What's more, there is always some tantalizing yet no doubt salacious gossip that there is some sixth sense ... a supernatural sense. Well, we are pleased to reveal that there is indeed a sixth sense, and a seventh, eighth, ninth, and tenth sense. Perhaps disappointingly, none of them are supernatural, and it is simply that the widely accepted classification of the senses is out of date. In fact it was Aristotle who gave us the archaic five senses, though the sheet-wearing beardy declined to include perceptions of pain, balance, motion, time, temperature difference, and perhaps even a weak magnetic compass locked up in that head of yours.

HOODED SEAL

CYSTOPHORA CRISTATA

❦

This smashing chum is much like any other seal: likes his fish, hates sharks, likes his ladies with a bit of meat on their bones, can inflate his head to twice its size while forcing an enormous scarlet balloon out of his nostril … hang on …

Lolling around the ice floes of southeast Hudson Bay you'll find the hooded seal. Once a year the females haul themselves up onto the ice to give birth, and of course to be ravished once more. Meanwhile the males will come and flop around next to them, waiting for the moment when the ladies forget what a pain all that childbirth was and fancy a bit of nookie again. The new moms, before any of that nookie nonsense begins, will nurse their young pup with milk for as little as four days—the shortest lactation period of any mammal. Incredibly, the pup doubles in size within the space of 96 hours. This could be something to do with the milk being 60 percent fat, which is almost the same fat content as a full English breakfast.

All peculiar stuff, but let us get around to that downright jolly bizarre nose balloon. The balloon is simply a message to other males that this young lady is spoken for and would he mind awfully moving on? The scarlet sac that pops out of one of his nostrils is a demonstration of his size and virility—a way of saying "Actually, you really don't want to take me on, old bean." It is safe to say that most animals really

◄ A hooded seal inflating his head and nasal membrane—a sight that naturally drives the ladies wild with desire.

▼ The hooded seal is found in the central and western North Atlantic. You will not miss them, I assure you.

The elephant seal, while looking like an affable fellow, is always ready for a fight.

would rather not get into a fight and risk getting hurt themselves and therefore not be able to mate—that would be dreadful—so the males weigh each other up, and if our friend looks certain to win the other fellow walks away. Of course, if he doesn't then it may well be time for a bit of a scrap. This is how many animals have evolved handy measuring devices to make sure they don't get into said scrap and waste all that precious energy and perhaps risk injury or even death.

Hit and Miss

Animals in general won't kill each other unless they consider their opposite to be cuisine. While our nature is rather more complex than that of our furry chums, we also will do our best not to hurt one another. The most remarkable example being the study of World War Two soldiers by Brigadier General S. L. A. Marshall. He found that an extraordinary 85 percent of troops were purposely aiming to miss, with only 15 percent aiming to kill. Incredible as it is, it is a comforting thought. Sadly, Marshall's discovery was used to shape modern techniques to mold a soldier's psyche and now 99 percent of soldiers shoot to kill.

While human nature is far too complex to put this kindness down to trying to stay alive to get females in the sack, it is nevertheless comforting to know that it is deep in our genetic make-up not to hurt one another. Another fine example being the Trobriand Islanders who have gone full circle and given up on the whole idea of war altogether and instead stage cricket matches. How devilishly civilized.

Male–male competition is basically combat, though rather sensibly many males have developed a way of signaling who is going to be best in a fight, which tends to be a show of strength or size. These appeasement rituals—including the hooded seal's inflatable nose—are really rather common in nature. Modern warfare, with its advanced technology, permits humans to kill each other from great distances, whether through the sights of a sniper rifle, or at the push of a button. Why is it so easy to kill someone in this manner? Well, because we don't look them in the eye anymore; we don't see the face of the human who doesn't want to be killed; we've removed the human appeasement ritual.

"If I could rearrange the alphabet, I would put 'U' and 'I' together."

The hooded seal attempting to impress a girl. Though his methods may be bizarre they are not half as bad as his chat up lines.

AYE-AYE

DAUBENTONIA MADAGASCARIENSIS

A primate that eats like a woodpecker, finds its way like a bat, and some say will stop at nothing to kill you in your sleep … sounds like a case for The Proceedings if ever there was one! Looking like he's terminally surprised and wildly gesticulating about something that's behind you, the aye-aye is a rather apt example of how evolution fills those nooks and crannies.

You see, the aye-aye is a woodpecker. OK, it is obviously not a woodpecker, but as there aren't any woodpeckers in Madagascar, this chap has evolved to fill that niche. He goes from tree to tree and with his long bony finger taps the bark to see if there are any grubs in there. If there are any tasty morsels he makes a hole, much like woodpeckers do elsewhere in the world, and uses said long bony finger to pick them out.

No one knows where the aye-aye got his name. Some say that it is onomatopoeic, as he makes a sound like his name, in much the same way as a cuckoo or a gecko. Indeed, many onomatopoeic names have been lost to time; "bleat" is the old English word for sheep and *brekekekex koax koax* is ancient Greek for marsh frog. Others say it comes from the Malagasay word *heh heh*, which means "I don't know," and that when early Europeans arrived on the island and asked what that particular animal was, the locals said they didn't know. A similar hypothesis exists for the South American llama; when Spaniards arrived

The aye-aye fills the role of a woodpecker in Madagascar. Instead of using a pecker he chews a hole in the bark and inserts his long fingers.

The population of aye-ayes is hanging on by the nails of their long bony fingers in the eastern Madagascan rainforest.

and wondered what the blazes those sheepy giraffey things were they asked the locals *Cómo se llama?*—"What is it called?" The natives, not yet speaking Spanish, quite reasonably surmised that these new mustachioed tall pointy-nosed strangers must call them llamas.

The wholly unrelated striped possum of Australia and New Guinea also spends its time with a big pointy finger bothering bugs in trees. He is very shy and little is known about him other than that he can be tracked by his noisy eating habits.

Finger Food

So the world's largest nocturnal primate wanders through the woods tapping away. Interestingly, they are the only primate that uses echolocation to get around ... a monkey-bat as it were. Aye-ayes have recently been observed to be rather affable fellows, with the males socializing happily at the edges of their territory. They are, however, less gentlemanly when it comes to sex and have been observed pulling other males off mid-bonk so that they can have a go. Aye-ayes are also somewhat fearless, and will happily wander right up to humans. This fearlessness, coupled with less than dashing looks, is often his downfall as the natives have grown to fear him. Often regarded as a witch and a symbol of death, it is said by some tribes that if an aye-aye points to you, it means you are about to die, and the spell can only be broken by killing the hapless creature. Other tribes go as far as to say that the aye-aye creeps into camps at night and pushes his finger into your main artery like a deadly silent assassin.

There is a flip side to all this superstitious mumbo-jumbo: the natives avoid the aye-aye like the grim reaper himself. Which means hopefully he can wander through the forest at night, squeaking like a bat and tapping away with his finger like the funny-looking woodpecker that he is.

Niche

The word comes from the Middle French for "nest" and refers to the particulars of where, when, and how a species fits into its environment—what it eats, where it lives, what it does to be different and keep out of other species' ways. One good example is the *Anolis* lizards, seven species of which can live in a small area of rainforest, all eating the same food. Each stays out of the way by living in a different area: some live on the floor, some on tree trunks, and some on branches.

The aye-aye constantly taps with his fingers at the bark trying to rouse any grubs. If he hears them he can then eat them.

"THEY ALSO MAKE TERRIFIC BACK-SCRATCHERS."

VAMPIRE BATS

SUBFAMILY: DESMODONTIDAE

At first glance, many take a dislike to the vampire bat, flapping around as he does, giving everyone the heeby jeebies and getting a load of free drinks. But give him a chance, dear reader; this flappy chappy actually always gets his round of drinks in … though he does seem to spend rather a long time in the bathroom.

The vampire bat is of course impeccably adapted to drinking blood. He will fly out only in absolute darkness to slurp on mammals and birds. He first detects his prey through the snuffling and snoring that we animals do when we sleep, and indeed the bit of its brain that deals with this information is rather pronounced—much like the part of Pilkington-Smythe's brain that locates booze. The common vampire bat also has thermoreceptors in his U-shaped nose, and once again his brain has a big bit in it—this time in exactly the same part that snakes use for thermoreception—so it would seem rather certain that they detect the warmth of blood rushing through bodies.

To get to all that lovely red stuff, unsurprisingly the vampire bats have big fangy teeth at the front, though it is not for the reason you would presume. First, if their prey is particularly hirsute, they use their teeth as a razor and shave the area they want to eat. Secondly, they nick open the wound and lap at it with their tongue. A substance in their saliva called draculin stops the blood clotting and, like a quiet night in our

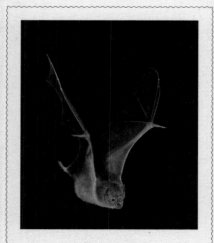

"I SAY, I'M OFF DOWN THE NAG'S HEAD IN CASE YOU FANCY A SWIFT ONE?"

A vampire bat flying out into the night to try to get himself a drink.

Vampire bats are much more likely to be found across Central and South America than in Transylvania.

local pub, they proceed to drink up to half their body weight. Of course, this is where going to the toilet rather sharply comes in handy, especially for a super-light flying mammal, a liquid lunch being frightfully heavy-going, you see. It quickly gets the wet bit of the blood and bundles it out of the back door via the kidneys. In fact, a common vampire bat's digestive system works so quickly it will begin wizzing within two minutes of starting to feed.

"HMMM, I'D HAVE GONE FOR A BIT MORE GARLIC IN THIS ONE OLD BOY."

Thermoreception

Most big animals feel temperature through their skin, though a few critters have managed to develop an ability to "see" heat. The pit viper and boa have sensory organs that tell them if anything nice and warm is nearby. The amazing possibility that the vampire bat is able to find animals by their body heat is tantalizing, although not exactly reassuring news.

Most creatures don't like being shaven in the night, especially if it leads to having their blood drunk and being wizzed all over. So it won't be a surprise to discover that sometimes vampire bats don't get a delicious bloody meal. Quite often, a vampire bat will go home empty-bellied. Not a problem, though, as when they arrive back at the big spooky castle they live in ... what ... don't they? How disappointing. Once they arrive back at the dark tree stump they call home, the ones who haven't got a meal will go and ask for one from the neighbor ... yes, like borrowing a cup of sugar ... as they may well die without getting a feed. All very well, if indeed the idea of vampires vomiting blood into each other's mouths is all very well, as it would seem that these bats are rather kind, friendly, and neighborly after all. Some learned types decided to do an experiment to see if bats would always share their spoils, and it turns out that there is a catch. They will stop sharing with a bat if that bat stops sharing the blood he collects. So vampire bats will only shout you a drink if you shout them one back. The moral of the story: don't be nice to anyone. Gadzooks, that can't be right—be nice to vampires ... nope ... always urinate when drinking half your body weight ... closer ... dammit, just be nice.

Fact

Reciprocal altruism, or as our less erudite chums know it, "tit for tat," is simply the concept of being nice to someone in the knowledge that they are going to be nice to you back. Vampire bats are a classic example, as are cleaner fish (saber-toothed blenny, pp. 64–5), and warning calls in monkeys. Now, who wants to buy ol' Pilky a drink?

JERBOA

FAMILY: DIPODIDAE

The jerboas are a group of hopping rodents found throughout Asia and Africa, and include the rather marvelous pygmy jerboa, the world's smallest rodent. These desert bouncers, like a number of animals, have taken to hopping as their favored method of getting about.

At first glance this appeared to be rather silly until we discovered it is actually one of the most efficient methods of getting from A to B. Large elastic tendons allow the energy from one hop to be bounced into the next, like jumping on springs. The lesser Egyptian jerboa, for example, is able to bounce three feet (1 m) at a time, which is rather effective for dodging other desert folk who would like to gobble it up. However, it is rather inelegant and it is not a coincidence that hopping animals make dreadful waiters.

Jerboas are finely tuned to living in the harsh desert—not least insofar as he has adapted his behavior, spending the daytime out of the hot glare of the sun, deep in his burrow—of which they have a number. The burrow in which they snooze away

LEXICON

Deserts

They're big sandy buggers right? Wrong, surprisingly. There are a number of different ways of defining deserts, a standard being if there is less than 10 inches (250 mm) of rainfall per year. Biologists often think of deserts as places that are devoid of free water, meaning that all the water there is locked up and unavailable for anyone to have a good sup at. This includes, for example, frozen water. Surprisingly, the two biggest deserts are actually made of water, albeit solid—namely the Arctic and the Antarctic. The Sahara comes in third.

With their tiny forelimbs, huge bouncy legs, and enormous feet the jerboas are ideally suited to hopping around the desert. For these very same reasons it's not a great surprise that they make dreadful waiting staff.

the daytime is rather well hidden and has a plug that they close to keep nasties out. They have a couple of other burrows that they use to evade predators, moving in and out to confuse anything that doesn't think the jerboa is too cute to eat.

Pocket Rocket

Indeed, there is a train of thought that some animals have evolved to be cute as a form of self-preservation, especially when they are nippers—so dewy-eyed, big-pawed, and lovely that you want to snuggle up to them rather than chomp down on them. It may well be that we have put pressure on animals to become adorable, killing things we don't like the look of. Indeed, it appears to be the way the conservation movement works, spending vast amounts of money on keeping nice-looking animals on the planet. Then there are other learned types who say that it is just a coincidence that these animals look like our young, and that we are genetically programmed to love our big-eyed pot-bellied offspring as they vomit, poop, scream, and generally just act all inconvenient through the first ten years of their existence. Either way, the pygmy jerboa comes out tops on the patented Proceedings of the Ever so Strange Cute-o-meter.

Still, a lot of the jerboas' outrageously exaggerated ears, noses, and generally adorable bits and pieces are rather fine adaptations to the big dry desert. Their enormous feet are covered in hairs that act like a pair of snow shoes to stop them from sinking in the desert sand. Many estivate, which is a lot like hibernating … only this time to avoid the harsh summer sun. Some jerboas never drink; they get their water from the food they eat, which sounds like a dreadful existence if you ask me. Still, if you did buy it a drink the lovable bouncing oaf would probably just spill it.

The jerboa can be found bouncing around the deserts of Africa and Asia.

The largest rodent is the capybara. Bigger than a labrador retriever, this enormous cousin of rats and jerboas is found in the swamps all across the continent of South America. Remarkably, its semi-aquatic lifestyle has led to its classification as a fish by the local Catholic church, so that the natives can have a big rodenty roast-up even during Lent.

Fact

"MIGHT I SUGGEST THAT SIR TRIES ANYTHING BUT THE FISH FROM THE MENU TODAY?"

MONITO DEL MONTE

DROMICIOPS GLIROIDES

—◆◆◆—

The tiny and really rather lovely monito del monte doesn't go around the world proclaiming different types of fruit to be in tip-top condition, nor is he "the little monkey of the mountain" as the natives like to call him. This chap could be the biggest case of a "missing person" in the animal kingdom; indeed the little expatriate was thought to be extinct more than eleven million years ago, before popping up in South America.

"I BLOODY LOVE STICKS, I DO!"

Forty-six million years ago, when India was colliding with Asia and causing the Himalayas to rise up out of the earth, the mega continent Gondwanaland was breaking up. At the same time, the monito del monte and the Australian marsupials diverged, and as the continents cracked apart, the little Australian was marooned on a small corner of South America.

There are of course those South American marsupials—the mammals that have a handy little pouch in front to keep their young and pocket watches in—namely the opossums and the shrew opossums. However, it seems the lovable monito del monte is actually a lot more closely related to the Australian marsupials: the kangaroos, wallabies, wombats (p. 187), and other rapscallions. Not so long ago in Queensland, Australia, there was a rather amazing find: a pretty little ankle bone and an ear bone. Small they may have been, but their significance is enormous. They belong to a tiny and rather incredible thing called *Djarthia*, which to all intents and purposes was a monito del monte. In fact they represent the oldest marsupial from Australia, the ancestral mother of all Australia's marvelous and curious creatures. Which means the little mountain monkey is a rather important formerly extinct tiny fellow. The monito del monte is the Aussie marsupial's mom, though don't tell them, as they'll all be over for a holiday.

 Remarkably, this chap appears to be the granddaddy of the kangaroos.

 This wee Australian can be found in the mountains of southern Chile. Do stroll over and say g'day.

There are of course many species that seemingly went extinct, only to suddenly appear feeling right as rain in some hitherto unexplored part of the planet. Such Lazarus taxa, as they are known, are perhaps inevitable as we know so little about the planet we live on. As we find new places and catalog new things, the odd anomaly will occur. Incidentally, these rediscovered chaps sometimes turn out to be impostors— new species that look like old species. These look-alikes are known as Elvis taxa … yes really, I'm not making it up. Furthermore, there are fossils that appear to go extinct and then are found millions of year later in the record— though they have simply been sloshed around to the wrong place, appearing as if they are walking dead. These are called Zombie taxa … now really, I must protest. I may be halfway through a rather nice Château Latour but yes, I am telling the absolute truth.

The monito del monte lives in a very small corner of the Chilean Andes, nesting in the bamboo thickets that grow there. He covers the nest with moss to keep warm and toasty, and will hibernate when the weather turns too cold. He eats insects and fruit—in fact the local mistletoe is so dependent on the monito del monte for seed dispersal it would quite simply go extinct if anything untoward happened to the little man … and we wouldn't want that to happen again.

Elvis taxon

One example of the Elvis taxa, as they are known in the plural, is the saber-toothed cat. Many creatures throughout history evolved honking great big saber-like teeth—*Thylacosmilus* and *Smilodon* are but two examples—though they evolved independently of each other. Such features may look superficially similar but this is merely an example of "ye olde convergent evolutionne."

(LEXICON)

Lazarus Taxon

There are many examples of lazarus taxa, a few of which are featured in this marvelous book. As well as the little monito del monte, you can peruse at your leisure the coelacanth (pp. 70–1) and the Cuban solenodon (pp. 176–7).

RIGHT WHALE

EUBALAENA SPP.

❦

Everyone knows the story of the right whale, the whale the whalers thought was the right whale because … well it was the "right" whale to catch. Well, I'll tell you something about this right whale fellow … he's just not right.

He is certainly an odd-looking fellow for starters. His huge mouth starts from way above his eye—a gaping maw chock full of baleen to strip the water of tasty shrimp and the like. On that head are big callosities, sometimes appearing white because of the huge lice that congregate on them. Indeed, what shoves this fellow clicking and squeaking into this collection is what is on the inside.

When you are dealing with whales it is not exactly a huge leap of the imagination to realize that you will encounter some big body parts, though there is one body part in particular that is really rather outsized. You see they have enormous gonads … balls … family jewels … call them what you will, one thing you can call them is bloody enormous. Each one is 1,100 pounds (500 kg), and together they weigh the same as a family sedan, though you wouldn't want to clamber inside one for a family day out, I'd warrant.

The fellows need them too, because the female right whale is something of a strumpet. When it comes to the mating season, the female right whale will take on multiple partners at the same time. They are tremendously sensuous creatures and it is said that the pressure of a human finger can give them a knee-trembler … if they hadn't evolved their knees away, of course. The right whales meet for watery orgies and the males gather around to nuzzle and stroke the female for hours before getting down to some naughty business with the female. So impatient are the males that they will often throw aside all decorum and all

⟁ Ye olde naturalists had great difficulty drawing whales as they could only get a decent look at them when they were beached and thus contorted by gravity.

"I THINK IT MAKES ME LOOK FAT."

Right whales were the first whales to be hunted, in places where they were easily reached by rowing boat. The advent of huge whaling ships spelled disaster for the other species of whale.

"WE WERE HAVING A WHALE OF A TIME UNTIL YOU LOT TURNED UP."

go at it with the girl at the same time. After which they all agree that they have had a merry old time and then wander off to find someone else to have nuptials with.

Such salacious behavior is just one of the reasons that female right whales don't live in small towns and attend church; there are also the tricksy laws of evolution at work in the form of sexual selection. This rather wonderful theory, postulated by Charlie Darwin, is the reason that males fight like rutting stags and show off like pompous peacocks. But combat (see hooded seal, pp. 136–7) and ornamentation (see long-tailed widow bird, pp. 112–13) are only two aspects of sexual selection. There are other shadowy goings on to consider, one of which is sperm competition. Indeed, the never-ending tussle for more offspring extends to the sperm of these giants. The right whale has evolved massive gonads to produce lots of sperm, which is sloshed into the female. Put bluntly, the male right whale is buying lots and lots of tickets in a lottery. I warned you that these chaps just aren't right.

The right whale population was decimated in the early days of whaling as they had a number of characteristics that made them "right" to catch. These slow-moving, inshore whales are now constantly struck by propellers and crashed into by boats, which means that some species of this rather marvelous creature are down to their hundreds. Sad news indeed, and while it is debatable whether this whale is right or not, we at The Proceedings can certainly tell you when something isn't right.

There are three species of right whale: the southern right whale, the North Atlantic right whale, and some poor buggers who live off the coast of Japan.

LEXICON

Sperm competition

Sperm competition is another way that animals compete with one another to produce more offspring. It has many permutations: the male dunnock bird pecks out its predecessor's sperm before mounting the female, whereas dragonflies have evolved a penis like a bottle brush to scrub out their predecessor's love goo. Even humans have sperm competition and a man will produce more of a type of "blocker" sperm, like a defending footballer, if he suspects his missus is having a fling with the milkman.

NAKED MOLE RAT

HETEROCEPHALUS GLABER

No, this isn't part of an old man ... this is the naked mole rat. A sort of shaved rat, although it does have a few whiskers, so perhaps that should be a sort of badly shaved rat. Not that it's a rat at all, nor is it a mole, nor has it been shaved, come to mention it. It does certainly look like it has lost its towel, though.

These smashing rodents live underground in the harsh and unforgiving East African deserts. Quite right they are too; it is bad enough looking like a John Thomas ... staying underground in the desert ensures they don't look like a burnt John Thomas.

The naked mole rats are radicivores. Quite, yes, they eat radishes—well not the red root, but bulbous roots all the same. They are really rather frugal with them, too, and will chew a little at a time from the center, ensuring the plant doesn't die. They do, however, turn coprophagic once in a while, and believe me, you really don't want to know what this means. Oh alright, you want a clue ... well *copro* means poop ... and *phage* to eat. Told you. When you are stuck in a hole in the desert eating your own poop you can be fairly sure that these are your "salad days." It is hardly sitting on the lawn with a pot

> The naked mole rat, hopefully eating something other than his own poop—that would make him look disgusting.

"Disgusting doesn't do it justice. Do you think I can get a decent steak tartare around here?"

of tea and scones, though it is a life that the naked mole rat is really rather good at.

These ingenious rodents have made a number of adaptations to their rather unforgiving environment. They have an incredibly low metabolism, using up about 60 percent of the energy that a mouse does in its day-to-day business. What's more, they use very little oxygen and are perhaps the only mammal that never feels pain. This rather handy adaptation is thought to be due to the lack of oxygen in the tunnels, where the build-up of carbon dioxide in the animal's body would bring about crippling agony. Of course, living in a hole in the desert, eating your own poop, and looking ugly as sin are punishment enough for one animal, and quite rightly the naked mole rat has evolved not to have to put up with pain.

Naked mole rats are also virtually cold-blooded; unlike most mammals, they can only keep warm over a very short period of time and so will huddle together to get all snuggly and toasty, or descend deep into their tunnels to cool down. Their big teeth are used to dig the tunnels, around which they are remarkably adept at whizzing. Remarkably, the naked mole rat can run as fast backwards as it can forwards.

We think by now, dear reader, that you are starting to understand that these guinea-pigs-in-the-buff are rather odd fellows, though we still haven't revealed what is oddest about these oddballs. You see, the naked mole rats rather unbelievably behave like ants. No, they don't get into your jam sandwiches at a picnic—that would be hideous. Rather, they have a eusocial society. Remarkably, the naked mole rat colony has a big blobby queen who has all the babies, a couple of strapping young male rats to service her needs, plus soldiers and tenders of the young, not to mention up to 300 workers to dig tunnels and whatnot. On the face of it, this is really rather inspirational, with the whole family working together for the greater good. At least it is until you hear the anecdotal evidence that when two naked mole rats' colonies expand into each other's territory, they will fight like bejesus, with the victor taking the other colony's members. It doesn't sound like a nice family day out to me.

A The Damaraland mole rat is the only other known eusocial mammal. He is larger, toothier, and rather more hirsute than his naked cousin.

V Remember: It's an easy mistake to make but naked mole rats are not found in your pants; you'll be much better off looking for them in the horn of Africa.

Eusociality

This is the highest level of social organization in animals. Examples include the ants, bees, termites, and of course the naked mole rats, among others. Humans are generally considered to be a level below—the presocial, which might go part way to explaining why my issue of *Pipe Smokers' Monthly* hasn't arrived yet.

BAIJI

LIPOTES VEXILLIFER

—◆——∞——◆—

*The baiji has made a terrible mistake, which to be honest has only endeared herself
to The Proceedings. She spent tens of thousands of years evolving to live in a lovely river,
only for someone to screw up all her hard work in the space of a few decades. The baiji's home
has had such an extensive screwing that she's unfortunately one of the rarest animals
on the planet, indeed if she is alive at all.*

◀ The baiji's
tiny eye has
all but disappeared
as she spends her
days in the murky
depths of the
Yangtze.

"WHAT'S THAT? WHO THE DEVIL SAID THAT?"

The baiji is one of four species of river dolphin that have evolved
independently around the world. Its Latin name is *Lipotes vexifil-
lier*, which means "left-behind flag-bearer" … sorry, no idea on that
one. Though perhaps this lovely Yangtze River dolphin's oddest mon-
icker is its nickname "Goddess of the River." I'm not saying the baiji
isn't entrancing, I'm merely saying that this heavenly title seems a tad
incongruous. In fact, such a name can only really be relevant if it is
common practice for the Yangtze locals to deafen, poison, and generally mistreat their goddesses. Perhaps screwing over vengeful deities is
the only way to explain why the river is so bloody awful in the
first place.

Sadly you'd be
rather hard-
pushed to find a baiji
even in the Yangtze.

It is fair to say that, as the Chinese economy has rapidly
developed, the natural habitat of many of China's animals has
been badly affected. After millions of years of unadulterated

Fact

bliss in one of the most beautiful places on the planet, suddenly the baiji dolphins are faced with numerous environmental problems. Of course, the Yangtze is a clear example of this degradation. Pollution and hunting have increased the pressure on their already fragile population.

Now a huge center of commerce, the Yangtze is about as peaceful as a Beijing bell factory. This lovely dolphin wasn't always so incongruous. She evolved in a rather muddy river and so forewent the need for sight. While she gave up trying to squint her way through the sediment-rich Yangtze, she evolved a highly developed sense of hearing. Of course, not so long ago she was having a lovely time; her hearing was so acute she was able to navigate the great river quite happily. That is, right up until the moment the motor engine was invented. Now the dolphin's home has circular saws whizzing through it that leave the poor thing absolutely unable to see anything that might be heading towards her … including the circular saws.

What's more, the pollutants and other stuff sloshing downriver have all added up to make sure that this river dolphin is done for. The baiji is now so rare that she has been declared functionally extinct, despite someone thinking they might have seen one a couple of years back. Suffice to say the poor bugger has had it. Even if there are a couple of these dolphin goddesses left, the chance of them even meeting each other in the Hades-like depths of the Yangtze sadly seems really rather unlikely.

The river dolphin of the Amazon is another curious fellow. He is thought by the natives to be a shapeshifter that changes into a handsome young man at night to seduce the tribeswomen. The dolphins' actual life is pretty rampant too; the males are known to have sex together, including using each other's blow holes as orifices … the only known example of nasal sex. They will also try and hump the oceanic tucuxi dolphin that also inhabits the River Amazon.

LEXICON

Binomial nomenclature

The binomial nomenclature system—that is, the couple of funny words listed under animals' common name—was invented by Swedish botanist Carolus Linnaeus (1707–1778). It's a rather clever way of grouping which animals, plants, and minerals go with which. Naturally, since we are a highly evolved bunch of primates, it didn't take too long before things got silly, so just for the record, here are a few of The Proceedings' favorites: *Notnops, Tisntnops, Taintnops*—three spiders previously thought to be of the Nops family; *Hebejeebie*—a plant of the Hebe genus which proved particularly difficult to classify; *Ba humbugi*—a snail from Fiji; and who could forget *Eubetia bigaulae*—a moth with the binomial name pronounced "you betcha by golly."

The Yangtze, the third longest river in the world, and the least hospitable place if you happen to be a short-sighted dolphin.

PANGOLIN

MANIS SPP.

Meet the rather marvelous pangolin. This chap is quite the inventor. We are of course rather quick as a species to congratulate ourselves on how clever we are—we have made all sorts of canny things like paper and air conditioning, and toasters and mustaches, and echolocation and glue, and Velcro and planes, and soup—aren't we clever! Well, the pangolin is a much more marvelous inventor than any of us daft apes.

It shouldn't surprise you to find out that clever nature got there first for pretty much every single thing we think we've made. Wasps make paper and a gecko's toe is a Velcro so efficient it sticks to glass; the termite's mound has air-conditioning, eels are electric, fireflies make light, and hundreds of animals use sound to look at things. Nature has spent millennia solving the problems that we have spent the last couple of hundred thousand years trying to work out, so quite frankly we shouldn't be so surprised when we find out they've come to the same conclusion, before we did.

Now it is often said that the wheel is mankind's greatest invention, which is ridiculous as quite frankly it won't get you drunk for starters. We would like to meet the inventor of beer ... I'd like to buy him a pint. Still, there are lily-livered types who think the wheel much better, and it of course will not surprise you clever people to be told that nature invented the wheel a long while before man. The pangolin is named from its Malay name *pengulling*, meaning something that rolls up. You see, the pangolin can curl up into a round thing to protect itself, to crash down slopes, or even to stick a leg out and slowly wheel itself away from lions ... good show.

Pangolins—a type of anteater—are a group of eight species found across Africa and Asia. There

The pangolin is often said to resemble a walking pine cone, though he's not quite as nice to sniff, not least because of the glands near his bottom that can emit a terrible smell similar to a skunk's.

"That's a bit harsh, old boy."

A pangolin demonstrating a rather good way of not becoming someone's supper—rolling up into an armored razor-sharp ball.

Fact

There are a number of creatures that invented the wheel way before we had invented diapers, never mind were in them. Web-toed salamanders bounce down steep hills like a loose car tire in the Sierra Nevada mountains; Namib wheeling spiders hurtle down dunes in the desert like whirling balls of nightmare; and mother-of-pearl moth caterpillars can even power themselves, shooting themselves along at 16 inches (40 cm) per second, 40 times faster than the speed they usually tootle along at.

are many types of anteater and it may surprise you to find out that they are in general quite unrelated. When we think of evolution, more often than not we think of animals turning into different species, becoming more and more different, and diverging. It is not surprising that these species, when choosing a similar lifestyle in various locations around the world, can come to resemble each other. A prime example is that of the anteaters; the South American giant anteater, the African aardvark, the Australasian echidna (p. 179), and of course our friend the pangolin, to name but a few. What is more, this convergent evolution can work on many different fronts, including behavior, and time and again nature has invented a wheel escape mechanism. There are salamanders that roll, caterpillars that whirl, and spiders that trundle.

Anyway, back to that adorable wheel, the pangolin. This particular anteater is covered in hard scales of keratin—the stuff that birds' feathers, rhinos' horns, and our nails and hair are made from. This chain-mail made up of fingernails is rather effective, not least because each plate is razor-sharp. In common with the other anteaters, they also have a big sticky tongue which they shove into holes to drag out insects. They don't have any teeth and can't chew, so their ant food is mushed up in a gizzard full of stones and sand, much like a bird has. Furthermore, they are clever; it is said to be rather hard to keep them caged as they will scheme and connive until they wriggle themselves out, which cheered us at The Proceedings no end. So there we have it … the pangolin: one of the greatest inventors the world has ever seen. We told you he was marvelous.

This rather inventive chap can be found across Africa and Asia.

HONEY BADGER

MELLIVORA CAPENSIS

---

*This little gadabout really, really likes to eat honey, a bit like Winnie the Pooh!
The difference between this cutey and Winnie the Pooh, of course, is that Tigger's
best mate won't attempt to bite off your John Thomas.*

Honey badgers are small and stocky—rather similar in stature to
European badgers, to be honest. They are found across Africa,
Arabia, and India, although they were found as far north as Italy back
in the day.

If you ever see a honey badger on the loose, run ... run with all you
have, for she is the world's most fearsome animal. What's more, rumor
has it that her favored method of attack is straight for the family jewels,
although we have had particular difficulty trying to find research assis-
tants to ascertain this particular fact.

Another favored *hors d'œuvres* is a cobra (note: John Thomas-
shaped), along with other poisonous snakes. If it just so happens that
it gets bitten by one of its deadly meals, and yes we are talking about
the sort of slithery customer that could take down a rhino, the honey
badger collapses on the spot, has a bit of a snooze, and wakes up a

He's adorable,
isn't he?
Though it is a very,
very bad idea to give
this cutey a cuddle.

> The male honey badger only has to endure about three days of unbridled animosity until the female takes him for a partner.

Fact

During recent warfare in the Arabian gulf, local rumors began to fly about British troops releasing fearsome beasts as swift as deer, the size of a dog, and with a head like a monkey. You won't be surprised to learn that it turned out they were simply a local population of honey badgers.

couple of hours later. Of course, it is none the worse for wear and will pick up where it left off during snacktime. Sadly, no one has got close enough to the psychotic bundles of fur to see what incredible metabolic processes are going on … though they are undoubtedly smashing.

Badgered to Death

If a lion is daft enough to get a honey badger in its jaws, the badger can spin around inside its loose skin and start biting and tearing at the lion's face. Not surprisingly, lions rarely attack honey badgers more than once. Humans for the most part don't fare too well either. African bushmen say if a honey badger moves into your village … it is time to move out. If you would care to be disconcerted a little more, we can tell you that the little sods are highly intelligent; they have been observed using tools to get to prey … moving things around to get to whatever it is they want to chomp on, which is anything they please, to be perfectly honest.

Honey badgers only have a single cub; he will spend time with his mother either in a den or while being dragged around the arid plains, to learn how to be a complete git to anything that moves, until the big day when he's grown up enough to be a complete git all on his own. Sadly though, due to this low birth rate, warfare, and some rather unsporting practices of trapping and poisoning honey badgers, there is a genuine threat to the population, which they find really annoying.

Let us just reiterate … the last thing you want to do is annoy a honey badger.

> The honey badger can be found across Africa, Asia, and anywhere else that it bloody well likes.

NARWHAL

MONODON MONOCEROS

❦

Since the dawn of time there have been a multitude of stories of that magical beast the unicorn: a single-horned horse with a billy goat's beard, a lion's tail, and cloven hooves. Its horn was highly prized, and worth more than gold, which is not surprising as it was said to bestow magical powers on its bearer. Queen Elizabeth I was said to be particularly fond of her carved and bejewelled horn ... and it was said to be worth "the cost of a castle."

Now we know that these magical unicorn horns are actually the tusks of narwhals. "Aaaaw," I hear you cry. I know, but as exciting as it would be, the existence of a unicorn is about as likely as the existence of a fair-minded traffic cop. Bear with me though, dear reader, for this narwhal is a creature every bit as wondrous as the unicorn.

In the seas above the Arctic Circle these sea unicorns are found in pods of between ten and 100. The narwhal gets his name from *nar*, the old Norse word for "corpse," as his mottled skin is said to be reminiscent of a drowned sailor. All interesting stuff but it is pretty obvious that what propels this creature straight into this collection is his magnificent prong. At an incredible six to ten feet (2–3 m) long, the male narwhal's tusk is actually a tooth, like the tusk of an elephant. The tooth grows out in a spiral form, usually from the left-hand side of the jaw. In fact, the narwhal boasts the most bizarre teething arrangement on the planet, followed closely by the British Royal Family.

What is really interesting about this rather obvious appendage is that no one is entirely sure what it is used for. The most widely accepted theory, put forward by Charles Darwin, is that the tooth has evolved as a sexually selected characteristic, similar to the mane of a lion or the tail of a peacock. That is to say that there is no real practical advantage to it—indeed it may put the creature at a disadvantage—but it is an

"WELL, YOU HAD THE MAP..."

Narwhals wouldn't leave the Arctic for any reason ... they find it just magical.

It may be that the narwhal's tusk detects whether water is about to freeze so that it doesn't get stuck.

(A) Narwhals have a cryptic coloration: they are dark on top like the midnight-blue Arctic ocean and light underneath so they are difficult to see from beneath.

example of healthiness to the female of the species and the more impressive it is, the more likely she will allow herself to be ravished by its owner. Other theories include that it is used for jousting other males, which is very likely to be untrue. Narwhals do exhibit a tusking behavior, whereby they rub them together at the surface, which is thought to help establish who's the boss. They may use them as a probe to look for crustacea and other bits of grub, and it has even been suggested that they use them as a pick to break Arctic ice.

The Erogenous Bone

Recently some really rather interesting research has shown that there is more to these mysterious tusks than meets the eye. Learned types took an electron micrograph of the enormous extremity and found that it contained an incredibly large number of nerve endings—ten million, to be precise. To put that into context, the most sensitive part of the human body is the female clitoris, which has eight thousand, and men have half of that number in their John Thomas. So the narwhal tusk is an incredibly sensitive device, and we can only imagine what sort of information might be picked up by it. Further research will hopefully soon tell us, and whatever is discovered, it is bound to be rather special. A sense organ so sensitive it defies belief ... you could even call it magical.

It is very easy to dismiss beasts of myth and legend as being ... ahem ... myth and legend. Though many a yarn has been spun on flights of fancy, many a myth is based on reality. The dragon legends of the East could be attributed to the rather large dragons of Komodo, or the fact that China's deserts are littered with dinosaur bones, which for many years were ground down and sold as dragon-bone medicinal tea. Other bones gave rise to the tales of the Cyclops, namely dwarf elephant skulls from the Mediterranean that had a huge hole in the forehead. There were old sailors' yarns of sea serpents (king of herrings, pp. 86–7) and there were tales of the Kraken—huge squid that could drag boats to their doom, much like a recently discovered colossal squid, which is bigger than the sperm whale. Who knows what else lies in the abyss waiting to step forth from myth to reality?

"MYTH? I'LL HAVE YOU KNOW I'M A BLOODY LEGEND."

PROBOSCIS MONKEY

NASALIS LARVATUS

With a fat belly and a nose like a blind carpenter's thumb, meet the rather lovely proboscis monkey. Locals refer to these splendid creatures as "Orang Belanda" or the Dutch monkey. Not that they are known for their love of tulips and wooden clogs; it was the outsized schnoz, the fat pot-belly, and all round orangeyness, that reminded the Borneans of the early Dutch colonizers.

So what need for this stupendous sniffer? Well, it seems the lady proboscis monkeys find it rather dashing; the bigger the better. On average, the male's schnoz is about seven inches (18 cm) long, and the female's considerably smaller, although still big. If you were a male proboscis monkey, your nose would be about the same size as your foot, though what it would smell like is open to a number of punchlines. In fact, they are so big it may be that the male needs to move his nose out of the way to take a chomp on some food. As if that wasn't enough, their noses swell and turn red when there is some sort of commotion, and act as a resonating chamber to amplify shouting and to aid in causing a hullabaloo.

"Oh no, it's no problem, I just get someone in once a week to mow the nasal hair."

The proboscis monkeys live in the swampy forests of tropical Borneo and are really rather adept at bobbing around in the trees and wading around in water. They are even proficient swimmers. It has been reported that these monkeys have been picked up by fishing boats miles from land. The monkeys certainly seem to like splashing around in the wet stuff, and after a bit of a wade they will think nothing of having a bit of a wander around on their two back legs, one of the only non-human mammals to do so. All of which brings us rather neatly to a possible insight into our own evolution.

The proboscis monkey is incredibly tardy and often arrives late. Thankfully his nose often gets there on time.

"I DO LOVE WHAT YOU'VE DONE WITH YOUR HAIR."

A The Dayak were a fearsome tribe of headhunters from Borneo. They were also rather natty dressers.

There is the thought that we didn't actually evolve on the African savannah; that we are in fact aquatic apes. This intriguing theory could go at least part way in answering the question of why humans look so different from other apes. The others are hairy and favor walking around on four legs, while we prefer two, which, as it happens, is a very handy stance for wading. Another striking example of why we may be evolved from a swimming ape is that other aquatic mammals have more often than not lost all their hair. The dugongs, the hippos, and the whales are examples of this. Like these aquatic mammals, we have a layer of fat to protect us from the cold, while other apes deposit fat around their organs. What is more, we are streamlined; imagine a gorilla trying to do the butterfly—he'd barely be able to get the swimming trunks on, we'd warrant. Finally, we can control our breath, which is a prerequisite of speaking. The other apes can't, but diving mammals certainly can.

It is certainly a splendid idea, and the evidence is indeed interesting, as is the large amount of evidence that says it is just hokum. Some may say that this is a crackpot theory, but I say poo poo to all you naysayers; you don't have to believe it, just stick your big toe in to test the wet stuff. The water is lovely—very nearly as lovely as the proboscis monkey.

Fact

Undoubtedly intriguing as the aquatic ape hypothesis is, the scientific community is largely against this one. Hairlessness is more easily explained as an adaptation to get rid of parasites than to speed up swimming. Breath control came about at around the same time as we started speaking, and the blobby stuff around your belly is less in keeping with sleek whales and seals, and more in common with domesticated animals that sit around the house eating too much and exercising too little. Can't think why.

V The proboscis monkey can be found in Borneo, unless he smells you coming first.

BUSHY-TAILED WOOD RAT

NEOTOMA CINEREA

❧

This adorable creature is the bushy-tailed wood rat ... also known as the pack rat, the wood rat, the prairie flounder, or Steve to his friends. Though let's not get fooled by this fluffy little fellow, who is in fact ... a rat!

The bushy-tailed wood rat is quite the rapscallion, spending his days thieving to build a bloody big house. It is hard to blame the poor soul, as small furry things didn't really get dealt the best hand in life. They're more like a furry sausage. Every bird of prey, snake, lizard, cat, and many, many more toothy scoundrels find them to be a rather agreeable *amuse-bouche*. So small furry things have gone ahead and evolved ways of avoiding being eaten as they find it rather tiresome and annoying. They are quite often fast and generally holed up in a burrow somewhere. Not so the bushy-tailed wood rat; he simply builds a big house or "midden."

Ⓐ Bushy-tailed wood rats may be found thieving across the northwestern Americas.

The bushy-tailed wood rat has a rather naughty habit of filching everything in sight. Of course, thousands of years ago that would have been pinecones, twigs, and whatnot. Nowadays, if you camp a little too close to their midden, it could just as easily include your wristwatch. In fact, they are drawn to anything shiny, and will drop whatever they are carrying if something else grabs their attention. If you get one in your house you may find your family jewels replaced with a pebble ... no not those family jewels ... we are rather sure you would notice that.

Ⓥ The bushy-tailed wood rat, a rather pleasing little purloiner.

It takes more than a penchant for shiny things to get into this collection, however. You see, this chap was rocketed into the Proceedings when we discovered that he holds together these middens with his pee.

His urine sets rock-solid like a hard varnish, and we do mean rock-solid. Some piss palaces have been found that are 40,000 years old, which is rather handy as these middens full of pilfered items can tell us a lot about how an area has changed over the centuries. I would write more about this fabulous rat but some knave's stolen my pen.

SLOW LORIS

NYCTICEBUS SPP.

She may look cute and cuddly but the slow loris is a vicious brute. Yes, she is kind of adorable, we know, but behind those big eyes is a merciless sociopath ... no really ... she has killed humans and she will kill again. Gadzooks, why won't you believe me?

These adorable villains slowly shuffle through the treetops at night, moving one limb at a time, presumably so as to not to clamber onto an unsuitable branch and plummet to their doom. They sneak up to any prey they can and with a lightning-quick lunge grab it with both hands. Slow lorises will even take birds and reptiles given half the chance. See, not so nice now, are they? But the worst is yet to come from these little rascals.

The villainous slow loris's most wretched characteristic is that she will not hesitate for a moment to slobber on her attacker. A dastardly and evil thing to do, I know, but the slow loris's drool contains a venomous liquid so powerful that it may cause slight swelling. But didn't we say she was a fiendish killer? Aaaah yes, we did hit upon the subject, didn't we! There is some debate as to whether the slow loris should be thought of as poisonous, as her poison was recently found to resemble the allergy thingy that a cat gives off. Do not let this fool you, however; it seems that some victims go into anaphylactic shock when exposed to it. Much like people who are killed each year by peanuts, it turns out some fellows are just very, very allergic to the slow loris. So there we have it, this adorable furball is as deadly as a peanut.

Sadly, they are hunted for their eyes, which are used in traditional eye medicines. Proof yet again of what remarkably intuitive and imaginative people traditional medicine makers can be. Coming soon to a traditional medicine center near you: ground-up elephants to make your ears and nose work better.

Fact

The pygmy slow loris was nearly wiped out by the Vietnam War due to the utter annihilation of the rainforest.

(▲) The lorises got their European name from the Dutch for "sluggish," or possibly from the older Dutch word for "clown" or "simpleton." There are no prizes for guessing why they have acquired the prefix "slow."

(▼) You can catch up with the slow lorises around southeast Asia.

BONOBO

PAN PANISCUS

This tremendous little fellow is often thought of as the "forgotten" ape Pan paniscus, *the pygmy chimpanzee. What this whippersnapper lacks in stature he more than makes up for in the trouser department, as these are possibly the most promiscuous creatures on the planet.*

Invariably when people speak of chimps they are talking about the bonobo's cousin the common chimpanzee, but this chap is actually a separate species that also lives in the Democratic Republic of Congo. The bonobo's appearance is slightly different—their legs are relatively longer and they find it easier to stand, and they have a darker face, pink lips, and long hair in a center parting ... is anyone picturing Queen Victoria right now or is it just me? The bonobo has evolved independently, south of the Congo, while its more famous cousins are found north of the great river, and it was only in 1939 that they were discovered, three centuries after all the other great apes. Incidentally, when early explorers first discovered the great apes of the Congo they assumed that they were in fact human and strolled right up to them to have a bit of a confab ... presumably to try to find out where they could find a passable gin and tonic in the area.

▼ Bonobos look altogether more human than the common chimpanzee. They are notably naughtier too.

"YES, YOU, SIR, ARE LOOKING AT A WANTON AND DEPRAVED EROTIC ADVENTURER..."

◄ You can pop by and say "How do you do?" to the bonobos in the Congo ... actually you might want to just observe them from a distance, they are a tad over-friendly.

"I Say!"

Right, on to the obscene. You see, bonobos like to have sex all the time: mothers with fathers, fathers with mothers, mothers with mothers, sons with sisters, sisters with sisters, fathers with fathers, mothers ... oh you get the point—basically everyone with anyone, with the possible exception of mothers with sons. What do you think they are, perverts or something? Like many animals, they are not afraid of a bit of homosexuality either. Male bonobos will hang from branches and "frot" or "penis-fence," or stand back to back and rub their scrotums together. Females on the other hand will "scissor," which doesn't require further explanation.

A pair of bonobos engaged in idle banter.

You see, in bonobo-world, having sex is just their way of getting along better and saying sorry. What is more, it is their way of saying "Hello, how do you do?" and "Isn't the weather much the same as yesterday as we live in equatorial Africa?" When you live in a tribe of a hundred horny little chimps that is a lot of bedroom athletics to get through. They even have sex when they find a new food source ... it is literally fair to say the bonobo have sex at the drop of a nut.

One more thing about this naughty chimp, and we can only apologize to all our lady readers for all this lasciviousness, but the bonobo is quite simply the only other creature on the planet that goes for face-to-face sex: tongue kissing and oral sex. Apart from a single pair of gorillas, that is, but all the other gorillas avoided them because they were a bit "funny." What is perhaps most human—and they really are "most human," being more closely related to us than they are to gorillas—is the bonobos' compassionate nature. Learned types have stated that the bonobo is capable of altruism, empathy, kindness, patience, and sensitivity. In fact, it is often mused that perhaps the chimps would be much better in the same genus as humans; *Homo paniscus* perhaps—or even we humans could be reclassified as *Pan sapiens*. Of course, no one has ever asked a bonobo what they would like; they'd probably have to have a think about it ... over a nice bit of monkey business.

(LEXICON)

Species

No one can really agree on what a species is, which isn't a good start when you have about a hundred million things to categorize. A common definition is a group of organisms capable of interbreeding and having babies of both sexes that are then capable of having viable little ones. Of course, there are plenty of species who don't need to be bounced around a mattress to make junior. What is more, a species may be a population that is isolated; lions and tigers can have babies, it is just that they don't run in the same social circles. Some see DNA as the way to go, while others think that a species has to look like each other, though we would wager they have never had a pet dog.

SPERM WHALE
PHYSETER MACROCEPHALUS

❦

We at The Proceedings of the Ever so Strange find the sperm whale an incredible beast. He is arguably the largest predator that has ever lived—a grumpy giant who is always up for a brawl. Remember that this is the chap who didn't go in for all that peace-and-flowers rubbish and fought back against the whalers. And we love him for it! Huzzah!

The sperm whale is so-called because whalers originally thought that the huge reserve of oily liquid in his head was actually . . . well, you can guess. It isn't, anyway. Its actual purpose is debatable and more than likely serves several purposes, none of them reproductive.

The oily goo is known to solidify when they are about to dive, so it could be to help the sperm whale swim at the phenomenal depths for which he is renowned. The enormous liquid-filled "melon" is almost certainly used as a remarkable 360-degree microphone, collecting information from miles around. Indeed, the whale uses his head to find food by echolocation and even makes the loudest known sound of any living species. He can reportedly click loudly enough to knock his favorite prey, the giant squid, off its tentacles—a sperm whale's special move, as it were.

There are many tales and legends about this incredible leviathan of the deep, notably that great work of American romanticism, *Moby-Dick* by Herman Melville. Melville's whale is rather a magnificent specimen, but few know that the story was actually inspired by true events, including the sinking of the *Essex*. When a huge sperm whale rammed the *Essex* twice, the ship took a one-way ticket to Davy

➤ This feisty bugger has a rather cosmopolitan distribution … because he wants to. Go on, try and stop him.

➤ Of course, at the time this was etched, no one had actually been batty enough to dive in next to a sperm whale to see what it looked like, so old sketches were at best approximations made from blobby remains washed up onto beaches.

"GADS, I FEEL TERRIBLE."

LEXICON

Ambergris

The mighty *Physeter macrocephalus* is one of the most cosmopolitan animals on the planet. No, they don't know how to mix the perfect Martini or have a commendable knowledge of jazz, but they are found all around the world. Moreover, they produce what was one of the most important additives from the golden days of perfumery: ambergris. You see, the sperm whale may be an enormous beast, but he is understandably squeamish about having to pass the beak of a giant squid through his system. To aid its passage, it is wrapped up in this ambergris stuff. Sometimes, alas, the beaks are just too big, so he has to vomit the oily chunk. The ambergris floats and after years of bobbing around the ocean acquires a sort of vintage whiff. What's more, it is worth an absolute fortune.

"Left a bit. Right a bit . . . Ooh, yes, that's got it. Smashing!"

Jones's Locker. The whalers were marooned on the Pitcairn Islands, where they ate everything in sight. Sadly, everything in sight wasn't all that agreeable; the salty diet gave them boils and lesions, and they became prone to bizarre and violent outbreaks. Of course, it wasn't long before they had eaten everything there was. They were soon drinking their own urine, and were half-crazed by cravings after the pipe tobacco ran out. In the end, they ate each other and were said to find jokes about karma deeply unfunny.

The Plum Predator

The largest animal that has ever lived (and here we include dinosaurs) is the sperm whale's chubby cousin, the blue whale. The blue whale siphons the sea for the tiny plankton that make up its diet, but does this make it a predator? Technically, yes, as they are eating animals, however tiny those animals may be. But we at The Proceedings like our predators with a pinch more callousness than a tubby bugger who ambles around the ocean with an open mouth in case something minuscule happens to float into it. May we also postulate that seeing as though plankton aren't actually able to get away, they don't really count as prey and the blue whale is therefore not a predator? Just a thought. So it may just be permissible to say that the sperm whale is the largest ever predator. It is, after all, bigger than the huge dinosaur *Spinosaurus*, which overshadowed *T. Rex*. It is bigger even than *Megalodon*, the enormous extinct shark, the fin of which is said to be the same size as a whole great white. Indeed, the rather magnificent sperm whale—the largest of the toothed whales—is a beast so tough that it will happily tussle with the London-bus-sized giant squid if it fancies a side order of calamari.

Fact

Other sources of smells for perfume include various shrubs, herbs, mosses, and the scrapings from a civet's bottom (see p. 186)—a creature that is said to look like a weasel . . . just a bit more miffed.

The Civet.

SIFAKA

PROPITHECUS SPP.

Meet one of the most dapper chaps on the planet. Granted he doesn't get his shirts from Brooks Brothers, nor does he know that a fine Harris tweed is of course unsurpassed as poor-weather attire, but he does know a thing or two about grooming. Say "good day" to the sifaka.

Sifakas are a type of lemur, a captivating collection of animals from the island of Madagascar—yes, home also to the aye-aye. Madagascar said adieu to Africa 90 million years ago, while dinosaurs were still skedaddling around the planet. The lemurs separated from the rest of the primates (you, me, chimpanzees, creationists, etc.) about 55 million years ago. They diversified and filled all the ecological niches that the lovely tropical paradise of Madagascar had to offer them, until man turned up and thought them quite tasty.

Their name is onomatopoeic; that is to say their name takes after the noise they make, like a cuckoo, a splosh, a quack, or indeed a zip. The sifaka, who despite being a dapper primate hasn't cottoned on

"How do you do?"

> ### LEXICON
>
> ## Adaptive radiation
>
> An animal may go down to the shops for a loaf of bread and suddenly find it is completely lost, so completely lost in fact that it is in an entirely new place where there is not even a relative to pop in to have a calming cup of tea with. It is quite possible that the animal will realize that this strange new place isn't too bad, and what is more there is a wealth of opportunities for an affable animal like his good self. As the years pass, all his kids and grandkids start to crowd the place up a bit. Not to worry, as they can begin to make new species and even take up new niches. It is this rapid speciation that is known as adaptive radiation.

The sifaka is legendary among couturiers for pulling off the near impossible "black tee shirt with orange pants" combination.

to onomatopoeic universal fasteners, lives on the western side of the island and makes a noise that sounds like "shee-fak," and so the tribes there call them "sifaka." On the eastern side, the sifaka make a noise much like a sneeze, and so the tribes there have given them a name that sounds much like a sneeze. Of course, this is mightily confusing for both the local tribes and the sifaka when it comes to the cold season.

While most lemurs like to bolt all over the place on all fours, the sifakas thought it much more refined to be a bit more ... well, upright ... and so are incredibly well adapted to bounding through the trees. In fact some hoof along at up to 20 mph (32 kph) amidst the twigs and branches. Of course, hoofing it through trees and being all stood up takes some skill. The sifaka manages this feat by leaping out from the trees, spinning 180 degrees, and landing back face-first on the next tree up to 30 feet (10 m) away. Being so well adapted to hoofing through branches means that they are rather ill-adapted to crossing land, though they do their best. Unfortunately, their best looks like a cowboy, heading towards the bar fresh from crossing the entire western plains on horseback after visiting the annual general nut-kicking competition.

"But why is he so dapper?" I hear you cry. Well it turns out that the sifaka has a number of remarkable implements at his disposal to keep himself presentable. He has a toothcomb—namely highly adapted teeth—that comb through his thick fur to keep himself clean. What's more, he has a toilet claw, which is used for ... what, it's not for ... for Gad's sake ... does that mean ... I'm so sorry for wasting everyone's time ... I thought it was used for ... oh, never mind.

Fact

Islands are rather special places to biologists. Not only do islands present them with something to stand on, but all sorts of tricksy evolutionary magic happens there, although a biologist's definition of an island tends to be a little broader than most. To these learned types, it simply means somewhere that is very difficult to get in or out of. An island may be a mountain lake, a steep-sided mountain, a valley bottom surrounded by steep sides, or an oasis in a desert. In some cases it may even be an island.

AN ISLAND.

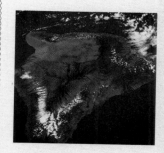

The sifaka can be found in his never-ending hunt for the finest sock suspenders in various parts of Madagascar.

PEN-TAILED TREE SHREW

PTILOCERCUS LOWII

———————◆———————

The pen-tailed tree shrew is one of the biggest drinkers on the planet. Of course, the biggest boozer on the planet is a disgraced member of the Pilkington-Smythe clan, but that is another story. An incredibly tiny drunkard this fellow is too. He is about the size of a small rat and remarkably manages to hoof down the equivalent of twelve glasses of wine every single night. Still, he doesn't seem to be too badly affected by going at it every night.

A pen-tailed tree shrew in a very rare case of being in his tree.

Upon ruminating on the subject, we are sure you will be as aghast as we are in working out that it really can't be that good an idea, if you're a teeny tiny tasty bite-sized beastie, to get absolutely hammered every evening. Predators would have the time of their lives, snacking freely on these self-marinating meals. Indeed, one of the very few studies in alcohol intake in animals looked at boozing in fruit bats, and whether they liked to eat fermenting fruit. They don't, and although we find it a rather large leap of the imagination, they're not silly buggers: "A drunk bat is a dead bat," as one of the researchers pointed out.

The pen-tailed tree shrew on the other hand frequents a rather affable tree, the Bertram palm, whose buds harbor a type of yeast. In the bud the nectar and yeast ferment, producing an alcoholic beverage. It is not just the pen-tailed tree shrew that has discovered this rainforest pub; seven species of beastie make regular trips to the plant. It is just our little shrew friend who is always there—the animal equivalent of the Pilkington-Smythes. The tree isn't daft, of course; it doesn't attract a gaggle of boozy animals to carouse around it and keep it awake all night for nothing. These little socialites act as pollinators. The Bertram palm and the pen-tailed tree shrew have been enjoying this happy relationship for nearly 55 million years ... yes quite ... the longest drinking binge in history.

Palm trees ... Sir Pilkington-Smythe's favored shrubbery.

Wetting the Whistle

Of course, man has long been boozing too. 12,000 years ago, when Stone-Age man was busy making primitive tools, he took care to make jugs to ferment fruit in. This was before he had the idea of baking bread. Some of the earliest writings from the Sumerians are in fact beer recipes. Indeed, alcoholic beverages were a safe way to drink liquid and not end up drinking a load of horrible beasties. While the pyramids were being built, the ancient Egyptians were supping on wines that were labeled by vintage and region. A thousand years before, the Chinese were making wine, which they believed nourished the soul. Some of our finest artists were dipsomaniacs; Twain, Hemingway, Beethoven, and Van Gogh were all inspired by a drop of the hard stuff. What's more, it's no great coincidence that our great leaders were big boozers and rabble rousers; Churchill was steamed pretty much all the time and John Adams was known to enjoy a beer for breakfast. Numerous religious rituals bear reference to booze, and when two souls decide they want to spend the rest of their days together we raise a glass to them. It's fair to say a drop of the good stuff is the very cornerstone of our civilization. Cheers!

Beer-making arrived in Blighty in the 16th century, making it the best century ever.

If you'd like to buy him a drink, you can find the pen-tailed tree shrew in a few locales.

GOLDEN-RUMPED ELEPHANT SHREW

RHYNCHOCYON CHRYSOPYGUS

Meet the golden-rumped elephant shrew, owner of one of the most magnificent bottoms in the animal kingdom, world champion skedaddler, and he is not even a shrew ... in fact he is more elephant than shrew.

The golden-rumped elephant shrew showing off his magnificent *derrière* (again).

"WHY, THANK YOU. YES, IT IS ONE OF MY BEST FEATURES, ISN'T IT?"

This lovely shrew and his smashing caboose can only be found in the Arabuko-Sokoke National Park in Kenya.

Despite having a big nose and looking a bit "shrewy," this fellow—like the rest of the elephant shrews and indeed the tree shrews—is not a relation. They don't even get a card from the shrews at Christmas. Yes quite, it is that fellow "convergent evolution" we keep going on about. It seems likely that the elephant shrews are closely related to the elephants, armadillos, and hyraxes, although even that is debated. Of course, the elephant shrews have been so called not because of modern genetic cladistic analyses to postulate phylogenetic trees, but because he's got a bloomin' big trunk on his face. He uses this great big nose to root around in the leaf litter looking for tasties, such as grasshoppers, beetles, and the like. It is a bit of a bother when he does actually manage to find something; to eat a worm he has to hold it with his foot, chew it on the side of his face (he has a big nose, remember) and then flick bits of worm into his mouth. No you are right, this little fellow is dreadful company to take out for supper, though a quite delightful companion in all other respects.

Pursuit deterrence

This is the rather amusing device of trying to goad someone who wants to eat you. Skylarks, when being chased by a bird of prey, will often sing—the message to the predator is "Not only can I outrun you but I can do it while bashing out a merry little ditty." Remarkably, it has been shown that merlins and the like give up the chase much quicker when the skylark is singing. I can't resist one more example of this demonstration of fitness: a type of *Anolis* lizard, when it spots a snake, will start doing push-ups. The message is "Not only can I see you, but I am in tip-top condition and ready for fisticuffs."

"Come On Then!"

It is not his lineage or manners that make this gentleman a real corker in this collection. Rather, he has evolved a remarkable number of ways to evade predators. First off, if the predator is far enough away, he legs it, and at quite a speed—as fast as 16 mph (25 kph), which is incredibly fast for such a small chap. If the golden-rumped elephant shrew is unfortunate enough to be too close to the predator, he does something rather unusual. Instead of keeping his head down and trying to hide, he does quite the opposite—he goes absolutely stark raving bonkers. The fellow causes a right hullabaloo, slapping the leaf litter to make a grand old ding-dong, and indeed to send a message to the predator, goading it to not to waste time attacking. This apparently works some of the time. An unusual method of predator-avoidance it may be, but this "pursuit deterrence" has been demonstrated a number of times and it is about showing that you are in tip-top condition, a "Come and have a go if you think you're tough enough" as it were.

In the event that this demonstration of fitness does not work, next up is "wonder-bottom to the rescue." His golden rump attracts attention, and as our hero scurries off through the undergrowth, the cad that is trying to eat him will have difficulty making a purchase on his bedazzling *derièrre* as it is rather tough and durable. The golden-rumped elephant shrew's bottom is so beguiling that the predator will go for it rather than the head, thus increasing the likelihood that the shrew will live. The third rather clever tactic to deceive predators is to maintain a number of different nests, thus helping ensure that each nest is not recognized as a food source by the hungry cad.

The golden-rumped elephant shrew: magnificent, we are sure you'll agree!

The hyrax is, surprisingly, a relative of the golden-rumped elephant shrew. Though it is perhaps a bigger surprise that he is more closely related to the elephants.

"I JUST HAVE A SHAKE FOR BREAKFAST AND LUNCH …"

SAIGA ANTELOPE

SAIGA TATARICA

Svelte and lithe, the antelopes bound across the plains of Africa and Asia. Delightful creatures they are too, but a few prefer not to hang around the savannah like a pretty meal ticket. There is the beautiful oryx of the Arabian desert, the adorable klipspringer of the Kopje, the majestic semi-aquatic sitatunga of the African swamps ... and the downright bizarre saiga of the Siberian steppe.

The critically endangered saiga lives on the remote Siberian steppe, though not because he is so self-conscious of his outsized snout. You see, that enormous nose is really rather handy out in the tundra. Inside it is very convoluted—as crooked as a line of Russian infantry—but as the cold winter air makes its epic journey through the saiga's nostrils it warms up ready to enter the lungs. In the summer, when the steppe is toasted by the sun, it gets rather dusty, and once again it is "wonder-schnoz" to the rescue as all those folds filter out the dust.

The incredible tale of how the saiga became so rare actually starts in Africa. The rhino, as everyone knows, has been hunted to near extinction for its horn—firstly by Sudanese males who used them as the handle for their *jambiya* daggers, and secondly for traditional medicine. Tests have indeed shown that rhino horns have anti-fever properties, a bit like aspirin or ibuprofen. Of course, some practitioners find popping to a drugstore to pick up a small pack for a pittance a

"PHNOT THE PHNELL NARR NEWW NOOKING PHNAT?"

The rather marvelous saiga and his rather marvelous snuffler that helps him survive the harsh conditions of the Siberian Steppe.

LEXICON

Antelope

The antelopes are a diverse bunch of even-toed animals dotted around the planet. They aren't necessarily closely related; they are more a hodge-podge of what was left over when naturalists grouped up the cattle, sheep, goats, buffalo, and whatnot.

bit of a chore. No ... no ... no ... it is much easier to circumnavigate the globe where said drug will be strapped to the front end of the second biggest (and grumpiest) land mammal—a big bugger who doesn't take kindly to being killed thank-you-very-much and will use said horn to protest about the whole shooting him dead thing ... all in all an absolute snip at about $10,000 a kilo.

Anyway, back to the snouty saiga who at the time were extinct in China, yet were found in droves across Russia. Indeed tens of thousands were hunted each year with no impact on their numbers. Then some "bright sparks" saw the commercial potential of the saiga's antlers, which have similar analgesic properties to the rhino horn, and decided these should be the new white gold. Given the increasingly affluent market for such things, the saiga population was decimated, from two million in the 1950s to as little as 50 thousand now. What fiend would do such a dastardly deed? Who would promote these wonderful creatures to be ground down by quack doctors? Unbelievably, it was the World Wildlife Fund—yes, the conservation charity the WWF. To be fair, it seemed like a good idea at the time; there were rather a lot of these saiga antelopes back then and it has undoubtedly taken the heat off the rhino, for which he is said to be rather grateful. Thankfully, now the WWF are now focusing their attentions on keeping this incredible chap and his magnificent schnoz on the planet.

Fact

There are a number of substances that allege to increase your success in the sack. Ground-down endangered animal body parts are not one of them. The benefit to the planet of keeping these rare fellows alive far outweigh the questionable benefits of quaffing their powdered remains. And the pharmacy is just so much more bloody convenient than the black market, don't you think?

During the ice age, saiga antelopes were found from Britain, throughout Asia and Alaska, and beyond. Sadly now they are only found in three little pockets.

Traditional Chinese medicine—if only it was as endangered as the animals it kills for use as ingredients.

ARMORED SHREW

SCUTISOREX SOMERENI

❧

At first glance, the armored shrew isn't much to look at; she isn't dripping in warrior-like shiny stuff, for a start, nor does she look like she'd be particularly handy in battle. In fact, to all intents and purposes it looks ... well, like a shrew.

The armored shrew is very normal: she is 6 inches (15 cm) long, brown and furry, has a pointy nose, and does shrewy things. But open her up and the first thing you will notice is that she doesn't take kindly to being opened up, thank you very much. The second thing you notice is that she has the most incredible skeleton.

Normally, mammals have five lumbar vertebrae, which are the pieces of spine that exist below the ribcage and behind the stomach. The armored shrew boasts an incredible 11 lumbar vertebrae, which is six more than normal. In fact, her skeleton is so complex it accounts for about 4 percent of her body weight, which is 300 percent greater than average for small mammals. This, along with extra thick ribs, allows the armored shrew to take an enormous weight on her back— the weight, in fact, of a fully grown man (around 155 lbs, or 70 kg). That is the equivalent of a human being bearing, well, 1,000 humans, which is of course not going to happen, not least because of the logistics, and because it would be rather unpleasant for all involved. What's more, in the same area they possess interlocking spikes that reinforce the spine while keeping it flexible. It is often remarked what a flexible little fellow the armored shrew is—it is said to be rather wiggly and snake-like and can quite easily turn in a very tight tunnel.

The armored, or hero, shrew, doesn't look very armored nor indeed heroic.

"COME ON AND STEP ON ME; I'LL SHOW YOU BLOODY HEROIC."

Shrews

Rather like the anteaters, the shrews are very often not shrews but are instead some sort of mischievous shrew-like imposter. It is all down to Europeans going around the planet telling natives that their name for a shrew is silly and wrong, and that they have those thingies back home so call them shrews. These shrewy impostors include the West Indies shrews, elephant shrews (pp. 170–1), tree shrews (pp. 168–9), and the otter shrews that are actually a type of tenrec (pp. 182–3).

A Skeleton in the Closet

These little shrews are revered by the locals who think them magical and will often take some body part of the hapless thing into battle as they believe it renders them invincible. Incredible stuff I know, but the best is yet to come. Quite simply, no one knows why the blazes it has this superb skeleton. Nature isn't brash and flamboyant, at least it isn't unless it gets you in with the ladies. She just doesn't like extravagances; why go to all the effort of making something that you don't need? Strutting around being all flamboyant is considered poor show in nature as it takes up a lot of energy that could be used to find food, or make babies with. Conjecture is rife as to why this shrew is like he is: could it be that he forages under precarious rocks? Is it a chance mutation that stuck despite a lack of selective pressure? Does she have a spine where other creatures use muscle? It seems likely that the armored shrew has gone to all the trouble of evolving to protect herself from "something" and then that "something" has disappeared from sight. Perhaps there's some elusive evolutionary pressure we're not being told about, although the nearby squashy-mouse-foot-stampy tribe assure us there's no such thing.

Of course, the idea of evolving to an environment and then that environment changing isn't anything new. Just look around you: hardly the subsistence living we hunter-gatherers have evolved for, is it? No wonder humans are chubby chocolate eaters about to keel over at any second.

Fact

Sometimes odd body shapes and bizarre behaviors can be explained by the "ghost of competition past." This isn't some competitive ghost giving everyone the heeby jeebies. Rather it is when an animal has evolved to stay out of another's way, and then the situation changes, leaving the evolved thingumajig looking peculiarly out of place.

The armored shrew lives in the Zaire basin, where you can go and tread on him if you want to.

SOLENODON

SOLENODON SPP.

———◦◦◦———

The "big-boobed poisonous mouse that couldn't walk in a straight line"
isn't a new children's book, but in fact a rather delightful creature from the
Americas—a creature whose downright dimness sets him apart from most other
mammals. Ladies and gentlemen, give a warm welcome to the rather
disordered solenodon.

◀ The solenodon:
one of the daftest
creatures the world has
ever seen.

"D'UH."

The solenodon is one of the rarest creatures on the planet. At one point many different species roamed across North America, but now there are only two left: the Haitian *paradoxus* and the Cuban *cubanus*. They really are incredibly scarce as they have been decimated by the arrival of man, and more significantly cats, dogs, and the introduced mongoose. Solenodons are simply just not cut out for being chased by these foreigners; the best they can muster in hasty retreat is an ungainly random waddle. Locals go as far as to say that they simply never travel in a straight line. If by some incredible chance their wandering off actually gets them away from a predator, they will go and hide by placing their head under something—yes, just their head—making this confused chap rather easy pickings.

Most mammals are really rather clever. They are fast to catch the most difficult of prey, like the mongoose taking down the cobra. They have complex communication systems and have self-awareness, like the dolphins. They are marvelously inventive, much like humans, who have made all sorts of extraordinary things like the gramophone, the Dewey decimal system, and alphabet noodles. Reptiles on the other hand are not known for their problem-solving skills; they haven't even worked out a way of getting around without having to lie in the sun for half an hour. Along with that other bunch of half-wits the arthropods, the reptiles have developed an overcomplicated and rather ineffective method of attack and defense … venom. It may sound rather incredible that a little snake or spider can deliver a bite that can take down a rhino in a matter of half an hour, but that is a long time to wait when dealing with a creature who is rather large and quite frankly more than a little miffed that you had the audacity to bite him in the first place. So it would take a phenomenally stupid mammal to develop such a bad way of attacking and defending itself … which brings us back rather neatly to our old chum the solenodon.

Solenodon means "grooved tooth" and it is this grooved tooth that she uses to deliver her poisonous bite. It makes her one of the only venomous mammals, along with that other ball of useless fur the slow loris (p. 161), and a couple of other waifs and strays. Still, the solenodon is rather magnificent and the world would be a much worse place if we were to lose her. One final point of note to shove the Solenodon firmly into the annals of the Ever So Strange: the female of the species has really rather unusual teats. They are very long and placed almost on her buttocks, and her spiky-toothed young will hang on to them and be dragged around for their formative weeks … which could go a long way in explaining why they are really rather long.

Fact

Mongooses are found across Africa and southern Asia, but it is the Indian mongoose that has decided to retire to other shores and generally cause a bit of a brouhaha in foreign climes. It was introduced to many places to stop rats eating sugar cane, and did a rather good job too. A bit too good a job in places in the West Indies and Hawaii, where they have chomped their way through a whole host of native and rare species, including the solenodon. Though the mongoose is a bit of a sod, it is really not his fault as he didn't ask to go there. One worthy note on the mongoose: while mating, the mongoose makes a noise called "giggling" and so may be the only species that isn't put off by giggling during intercourse.

"I WAS GIGGLING DEAR, I WASN'T LAUGHING."

These daft buggers can be seen ambling around in Haiti and Cuba.

SLOTH

SUBORDER: FOLIVORA

Meet one of the most affable creatures in the animal kingdom, though don't invite him round for high tea; he will arrive unbearably late and quite frankly has a sense of hygiene that would make a Parisian hotelier swoon.

The sloths live in the treetops of South and Central America. They eat pretty much anything they catch, which, given the fact that they are remarkably dawdling creatures, pretty much means leaves. Sloths hang in the trees upside down, trying to catch up with leaves, and if they do manage to get close they will pounce or amble—whichever is slowest—and scoff them down. With his belly full he is ready to face the day with all sorts of apathy, and can stroll along to try to catch more static objects.

The sloth's fur is teeming with life, like a little rainforest within the rainforest. His hairiness is chock-full of algae-like bacteria, making the sloth appear green; he also has a merry menagerie of mites, ticks, and beetles. There are also moths that live in the fur and lay their eggs in the poop that the sloth expels once a week.

Despite their slovenly habits, they are rather a successful bunch. No, they haven't built up a fleet of small businesses across the British Empire. Instead, they are very well suited to their arboreal existence. In fact the sloth can make up two thirds of the mammalian biomass of a forest area. They are largely unfussed by predators too; the little ecosystem covering them takes care of that problem, keeping them well camouflaged, meaning the sloth's friends all get to live on another day. I told you they were affable fellows. Perhaps we should have them round for tea after all.

"No ... no ... gluttony and envy are in the next tree along."

If he can't make it for tea you should go round to his part of the woods, he's very accommodating.

ECHIDNA

FAMILY: TACHYGLOSSIDAE

*What the blazes have we got here, then? Despite looking like some
nonsense-creature dreamed up by rakish medieval naturalists of yore,
this lady is bona fide. She may look like a kiwi crossed with a toilet brush,
but she is rather more bizarre than many a mammal.*

The echidna
can be found
behaving oddly in
various locales;
namely Australia and
New Guinea.

The echidna lays eggs like a bird, has a pouch like a kanga-roo, and feeds her young with milk like a mammal, making this beaky spiky milky creature a rather special addition to the collection. The echidnas, both short- and long-beaked, along with the duck-billed platypus, make up the three surviving monotremes. These monotremes (meaning "one hole") are so called because they have a cloaca. The cloaca, as discussed previously, is used to drop everything out: waste, babies, and whatnot. Having said that, a cloaca is not the only thing this curious bunch have in common with birds. These mammals actually lay eggs—a rather odd behavior from our warm-blooded brethren until we note that their young puggles—yes their young are called puggles—are fed with milk.

The breeding rituals of the echidnas are really rather magnificent. Once a female is nearly ready to take a mate she begins emitting pheromones that are irresistible to the males, and for over a month a train of wanton suitors begin to follow her around. This convoy of up to eleven males will trot along after her until the day she finally decides she is ready for some action. A fracas forms among the males, and they gently jostle each other for hours, all the while creating a deep donut-shaped trench around the female. Eventually, when a winner is decided, the game female moves into position and the winning suitor unsheaths his four-headed penis, ready for nuptials.

All of which raises the question why, with animals so bloody bizarre, the medieval naturalists felt the need to invent animals. It defies belief.

"ALRIGHT, WHO CALLED ME 'FUNNY LOOKING'?"

TAPIR

TAPIRUS SPP.

❦

It has to be said that this remarkable fellow, the tapir, just doesn't look right.
The closest approximation that we at The Proceedings can give is some kind of a
cross between a pig and an elephant. Of course, crossing a pig with an elephant isn't
recommended—at best you would get a squashed pig. Thankfully our little
impossible creature the tapir is very possible.

The four species of tapir form an odd hodgepodge of creatures and are the last bastions of a once great and diverse bunch of nosey animals across the globe. The species are the Baird's tapir in Central America, the mountain tapir of the northern Andes, the Malayan tapir, and the Brazilian tapir. There were once tapirs everywhere; now sadly there are just lucky little pockets left.

The tapir are quite large—roughly in between the size of a sheep and a cow—and are related to the horse and the rhino. The young have a remarkable coloration pattern as they are mottled to mimic the effect of dappled sunlight on a forest floor, much like a watermelon's camouflage. Indeed, it is very hard to look at one without wanting to gobble up the really rather lovable oaf. The adults are brown, with the exception of the Malayan tapir, which has a white saddle on a black

◀ This rather unusual chap is the Brazilian tapir, and we think he's smashing.

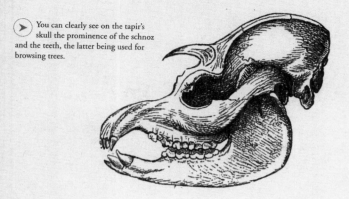

➤ You can clearly see on the tapir's skull the prominence of the schnoz and the teeth, the latter being used for browsing trees.

There are quite a lot of extant species (species that are still alive). Somewhere between five and 200 million species are busy just being alive right at this very moment in time. Of course, that is a rather puny—not to mention vague—number when you look at all the species that ever existed. In fact, the 1–200 million species alive today are thought to be only one percent of all the species that have ever existed.

background. Although it looks like it is doing a terrible impression of a penguin—an animal renowned for its inability to blend into Southeast-Asian rainforest—it is actually rather well camouflaged. The predators of the area tend to see in black and white, and the stark contrast manages to break up its outline.

Despite all this, I think we all know what has got this animal an entry into this book … it is that great big sniffer of his. Actually, it is probably safer to call it a short trunk, and it is used for browsing the trees and plants for food. Yes quite, that is where we get the word from (see box); some herbivores browse the trees and others graze on the ground. That is not all this wonder-nose is used for. Obviously, it is used for smelling, but it is also rather smashingly used as a snorkel. Tapirs love to have a swim and submerge themselves like a cute furry submarine. There are plenty of good reasons why they like doing it, too; it is nice and cool and the fish can nibble off any parasites. It is even a form of defense—should a predator manage to latch on to this chap it will have difficulty getting a purchase on the tough ridge along the back of his neck. Rather splendidly, it is said that if they are caught they jump into the nearest bit of water, carrying the predator to the bottom. The tapir is perfectly happy deep in the drink, but the predator really doesn't like it and quite understandably lets go. Huzzah!

(LEXICON)

Browsers and grazers

Browsers eat the leaves from trees and bushes, whereas grazers eat grasses and whatnot from the floor. Animals evolve to be rather good at it, too, adapting to whatever it is they fancy for lunch. Good examples are sheep and goats; though closely related they look rather different.

▼ Tapirs not surprisingly have an unusual distribution dotted around the New World, as well as parts of southeast Asia.

TENREC

FAMILY: TENRECIDAE

Hurrah! We at The Proceedings doff our caps to this intriguing creature. Yes, quite ... he does look like a rather dapper hedgehog, but in fact he is no relation whatsoever. His closest relatives are the golden moles, elephants, and hyraxes, which makes choosing a suitable venue for family get-togethers really rather awkward.

> Many tenrecs look just like hedgehogs, though they are quite unrelated.

"I'M NOT A HEDGEHOG—I'M VERY HAPPY TO SHARE THE HEDGE."

Tenrecs are a flabbergasting bunch. There are 30 species of them dotted around Madagascar and South Africa. They inhabit a number of different ecological niches; some favor bobbing around in rivers, others scrabbling around in bushes, some are up trees and others live underground. Remarkably, they have grown to look quite a lot like some rather more familiar species. Some are the spitting image of a hedgehog.

Others are well adapted to water and look like otters. Others bound around bearing a remarkable resemblance to tree shrews. The lowland streaked tenrec appears to have evolved to look like an overdressed dandy.

Talking Balls

Time to talk balls, more so than usual, because these gentlemen lack them. They have testes of course, but they are one of the few mammals that keep them inside their body. Testicles as you know produce sperm and hormones, for mating and producing "maleness" in the body, including facial hair, libido, and propensity for pipe-smoking. As the testes don't work very well in the hot temperatures inside the body, most animals have balls that hang out of the body. A few animals, such as the whales and dolphins, keep them inside their body and have adapted elaborate systems to keep them cool. The tenrecs, being sensible, just have a cool body temperature.

There is another odd body feature about them in that they have a single opening for all their intake and outtake. Their bum and other bits are one and the same—a single multifunctional hole known as a cloaca, which is more commonly seen in birds, reptiles, and amphibians.

So there it is! A quite remarkable and rather familiar fellow I'm sure you'll agree!

Tenrecs are found looking a bit like hedgehogs on Madagascar and across central Africa.

Convergent evolution

Evolution is known for branching off in a big complex "tree" leading to all sorts of curious creatures, including our nutless friend the tenrec. There are, however, only so many answers to every ecological problem. To live in the air you had better get yourself a good pair of wings or you won't be living in the air very long. Not living in the air hurts if you are a "living in the air" type of creature without wings, and so bats and birds look similar even though they are from wildly different groups. The group we call the anteaters are entirely unrelated, although they look the same because they tuck into the same type of grub. Tenrecs look like hedgehogs, tree shrews, and otters because they live like hedgehogs, tree shrews, and otters.

The lowland streaked tenrec is obviously in the same niche as a musical theater group.

GELADA

THEROPITHECUS GELADA

The geladas are a bunch of hairy Old World monkeys from the Ethiopian Highlands. We, it has to be said, are rather taken with them, not least because they have a number of quirks that remind us of ourselves.

Geladas live in the mountains of Ethiopia in huge groups, where they sit around for most of the day eating grass and grooming. For this reason they have evolved two rather human adaptations to their environment. The first is that next to humans they have the most advanced opposable thumb in the animal kingdom in order to pluck grass, which is their food of choice. The second is the big fat buttocks they like to sit on, though it is perhaps a more unusual, and rather racy adaptation that landed these fellows in our almanac.

It is also noteworthy that, along with humans, this is the ape that likes to live at the highest altitudes, although it is somewhat of a mystery as to why geladas like to climb to 14,750 feet (4,500m) above sea level as there is certainly nothing for them to gobble up there. The best suggestion we at The Proceedings can come up with is that they quite simply like the view. To show that they are frightened or submissive, geladas flip up their lip to reveal their

"Don't know why you find it so fascinating, funny face."

This rather familiar fellow graces the mountain meadows of Ethiopia.

A male gelada clearly showing the markings on his chest that are a representation of the female's genitals.

 The gelada has a number of facial expressions to let everyone know exactly what he is thinking.

enormous inci- sors, which con- versely is enough to give any other living being on the planet a case of the severest heeby jeebies. Indeed, a flash of the teeth is generally a sign of aggression in most animals, including the primates. One of the only other primates to give out these seriously misleading toothy signals would again be a grinning human.

It is the markings on their chests, how- ever, that really propel geladas into our menagerie. You see, the female's private parts are covered by her fat buttocks, and because she spends so much time sitting down, the male can't tell when she is ready to mate. So the lady gelada has evolved an exact replica of her lady-bits on her chest. These pretend lady-bits swell and blister when she is in season, which has been called "necklacing." Curiously, the male has also evolved these lady-bits shapes on his chest. Curious, that is, until you once again consider the human animal. You see, humans spend much of their time sitting around on their fat buttocks, not to men- tion hiding their shame with clothing. So they have evolved protrusions on their face ... lips we like to call them ... that mimic the female geni- talia, and even male humans have them.

LEXICON

Prosopagnosia

This is the inability to recognize faces. The most famous pros- opagnosic is primatologist Dr. Jane Goodall, which may go a long way to explaining why she likes chimps so much in the first place.

Baboons, Drills, and Mandrills

Geladas are related to baboons, and their close relatives the drills and mandrills. There are five spe- cies of baboon, ranging from the rather small guinea baboon that weighs in at a paltry 30 pounds (14 kg), to the huge chacma baboon that tops the scales at 88 pounds (40 kg) and has canine teeth bigger than a lion's. Bigger still are the related mandrill and drill. The mandrill has a very brightly colored face and is the world's largest species of monkey. The drill is slightly smaller, with a black face and a very brightly col- ored bottom that helps its family follow him through the forest.

"IT IS RATHER BEGUILING ISN'T IT?"

CIVET

FAMILY: VIVERRIDAE

A rather pleasant-looking chap is the civet: a cat-like fellow with perhaps a soupçon of the otter or mongoose. What is more, he has a rather delightful derrière.

U nfortunately for him, the civet is considered a delicacy by some people. Eating SARS-infected civets landed many a diner in the hospital, which has meant more bad luck for civets as they have subsequently been slaughtered in the thousands for having the audacity to be tasty and susceptible to disease at the same time.

Talking of tasty, those who know me will be aware that I'm quite the connoisseur and gastronome. I've eaten more funny things than the cannibals who discovered the shipwrecked clown ship. Once in Ho Chi Minh City I partook of the *caphe cut chon* beverage. Sadly my knowledge of French-Indochinese cuisine was lacking at the time, as you see this coffee is actually produced from civet excrement. They feed the hapless fellow (who it should be noted much prefers a cup of tea anyway) coffee fruit. Out pop the beans a couple of days later.

One final thing about this splendid creature is that he has made an incredibly important contribution to perfumes. You see, that clever little bottom of his contains a set of perianal glands that secrete a high-quality musk with a smokey aroma. The musk is collected with a scraping spoon, which is in no way pleasant for the poor bloody civet, and he is said to have developed quite an aversion to silver service dining. Still, it is rather nice-smelling. So there it is, the civet—the animal with the world's most sophisticated bottom.

Fact

The fossa, or Malagasy civet, is a formidable predator from the island of Madagascar. Looking like a cross between a sinewy mountain lion and a weasel, he feeds on the lemurs and other tasties found on the islands, where he stalks them in the fast-disappearing forest. The fossa uses his long tail as a balance, much like the big stick that a circus tightrope walker uses, and he is capable of explosive speeds.

The civet can be found in Africa and Asia, though don't talk to him unless he's had his morning brew.

WOMBAT

FAMILY: VOMBATIDAE

He really is quite a delight, isn't he? A lazy slacker at that! This slothful fellow likes to take things easy; he spends 16 hours a day snoozing away, while the remainder is a time for resting.

It comes down to the rather energy-poor food these chaps like to graze on. Thankfully they have such an efficient digestive system that they only need to eat about a third of the amount a sheep or similar grass-eater would chow down on. Incredibly, however, all the energy is so locked up in all that plant roughage that it takes 14 days for one meal to be fully digested. The rather wonderful wombats need even less water—about 20 percent of a sheep's requirement. This unbelievably slow metabolism is an adaptation to the arid, nutrient-low bush in which they live. It is also a handy excuse for why they just can't seem to fit into those britches anymore.

After this epic bit of digestion, our dawdling hero will poop out a cube of dung. Yes, absolutely … a cube. Wombats use their dung as a marker of their territory and it is thought that he makes these rather angular plops so that they don't roll away. Exactly how they do this incredible bit of bottom crafting even I don't want to know.

One last thing about this smasher: his bum is as tough as an old boot. If a wombat comes across a predator such as a dingo, he skedaddles to the nearest burrow—indeed he can be there in a jiffy as he really can motor. Once the wombat is in its burrow it is really rather fine and dandy—he blocks the end with his cartilaginous *derrière*. Hurrah!

As a wombat is a burrowing marsupial, the pouch in which she keeps her young is positioned upside down so as not to fill with earth as the wombat digs.

The wombats are found in three very lucky parts of Australia.